THE SECRET LANGUAGE OF MANIFESTATION

MAKING THE INVISIBLE VISIBLE

DENISE JARVIE
ARTWORK BY DANIEL B. HOLEMAN

The Secret Language of Manifestation
Making the Invisible Visible

Copyright © 2025 Denise Jarvie
Artwork Copyright © 2025 Daniel B. Holeman

All rights reserved. Except for personal use, no part of this publication may be reproduced, in whole or in part, without written permission from the publisher. These cards are for spiritual and emotional guidance only and are not a substitute for medical advice or treatment. The author's views, within and beyond this publication, do not necessarily reflect those of the publisher. We respectfully request that this content not be used to train AI-generative models or machine learning systems without the publisher's written consent.

Published by Blue Angel Publishing®
10 Trafford Court, Wheelers Hill,
Victoria, Australia 3150
E-mail: info@blueangelonline.com
Website: www.blueangelonline.com

Edited by Peter Loupelis and Cherise Asmah

Blue Angel is a registered trademark of Blue Angel Gallery Pty Ltd.

ISBN:978-1-922574-44-2

Printed on sustainably sourced paper,
with soy-based inks.

Dedication

Thank you
for being you.

We are a part
of all that
we have met.

Camera and recorder, within range of limits, can photograph and record without selection or distortion from a point of zero interference. The camera achieves a nirvana of uncritical acceptance. It rejects nothing, it clings to nothing, it fears nothing, it desires nothing. It hates nothing, it loves nothing. Camera and recorder are crude models of your own built in equipment. You can make your own movies from a point of zero interference, once you stop interfering, the movies move themselves. Why pay black mail at the box office? Why not make your own movies? You have all the screens you can fill and all the projectors you need. So, turn the zero camera on yourself, you never see anything else anyway.

— William S. Burroughs

ACKNOWLEDGEMENTS

Asherah, Astar, Na, and Koko: thank you for endless wonder.

Thank you to the most talented and hardworking team at Blue Angel Publishing. You make my work dreams come true.

Thank you to my editor, Peter Loupelis, who gently pushed me beyond what I thought I could do, allowing me to touch parallel realities that held the best version of this deck.

Thank you to Daniel Holeman for his light-filled art that brings healing inspiration to create new ways.

Thank you to my family and friends, whose endless love, support, and belief are constant inspiration and wonder.

Thank you to my clients and students — your love, light, and grace inspire me to be a better communicator and human.

A big thank you to Dave, my cat companion — a sweet, nutty, healing, interdimensional being who keeps me grounded.

Thank you to these physical and non-physical educators and writers that inspired this deck and my slice of the truth: Abraham–Hicks, Sanaya Roman, Dolores Cannon, Stuart Wilde, Paramahansa Yogananda, Matias De Stefano, Ken Wilber, Darryl Anka and Bashar, Lee Carroll and Kryon, the Sassanis, Pleiadeans, Arcturians, Sirians, and star beings from Orion and Vega.

TABLE OF CONTENTS

11 Welcome, Creative One

13 INTRODUCTION
15 The Language of Manifestation
20 The Path of Most and Least Allowance — Releasing Resistance
24 Your Manifestation Name
26 Conscious Creation Masterclass
29 Using the Cards as an Oracle
32 Manifestation Spreads

CARD MEANINGS AND CONSCIOUS CREATOR MASTERCLASSES
38 1. Manifestation Name
42 2. Waking Up
46 3. Beliefs
50 4. Gratitude
54 5. Wellbeing
58 6. Desire
62 7. Heartfulness
67 8. Meditation
73 9. Emotions
78 10. Soul Perspective
83 11. Remembrance
87 12. Alignment
92 13. The Principle of Attraction
97 14. Create Your World
102 15. Attraction Point
107 16. Vibration
112 17. Dancing with Your Rhythm

18. Nothing Happens by Chance 117
19. The Harmony of Contrast 122
20. Divine Feminine 126
21. Divine Masculine 130
22. Sacred Union 134
23. Abundance 138
24. Innovation 142
25. Visionary 146
26. Wouldn't It Be Lovely 150
27. The Prearrangement of Free Will 156
28. Picture Your Goals 160
29. Moon Illumination 164
30. Dimensions 168
31. The Source 172
32. Duality 177
33. Reality 182
34. Beyond Spacetime 187
35. An Elevated Perspective 192
36. Spiritual Alchemy 197
37. Illumination 202
38. Akasha 207
39. Beyond 211
40. Multidimensional 216
41. Nature Wisdom 221
42. Interspecies Communication 226
43. Alternate Lifetimes 230
44. Eternity 235
45. Passion Creator 240

About the Author 247
About the Artist 249

WELCOME, CREATIVE ONE

I am pleased and honoured that you are here. This deck embodies my desire to cultivate a loving, safe atmosphere that advances you through the levels of creating to become a conscious, highly attuned architect of your reality, across all areas of your life. Each card is saturated in variations of cosmic visions to inspire and clarify your soul's dreams and desires.

The path of self-discovery is a brave and liberating process. It begins with an expanded perspective that allows us to choose synchronistic opportunities. Then, over time, we realise life doesn't happen to us — it happens from us, and we are co-creators of our lives. You are creating your future in every moment of your life. Like gravity, we can't see how it works, but we experience the effects.

The messages, visualisation, journal work, reflections, and actions will initiate pathways into an expanded sense of genuine soul-knowingness where you can dive into an ocean of pure potential and swim through inspirational ideas that satisfy and fulfil your heart.

You can have or be whatever your heart and imagination desire. If you are reading this, you are well on your way. This life, your life, is an incredible adventure. Be kind, curious and dream big!

In love and creation,
Denise

INTRODUCTION

If you don't know where you're going,
any road will get you there.
—*George Harrison*

To manifest it is to attract something that resonates at a similar vibration frequency. Your desires create an emotional environment vibrating at a particular frequency, which becomes the basis for what you attract. You desire something because you believe it will improve your life. Desires are filled with dreams, wants, or needs that become a unique soup of emotions. The manifestation process echoes the emotional vibrational frequency, and you begin to experience the physical expressions of those frequencies.

As desires manifest, you can measure their validity and decide if you want more, similar manifestations. The expression "be careful what you wish for" implies that we can get this process wrong, which is not true. An outcome can only be revealed after experiencing it, physically. Being told, "You should have known better," feeds fear and creates procrastination.

Any experiences, people, or ideas you encounter become your baseline for choosing more of the same or something different. I urge you to try many ways to clarify and fine-tune your dreams and desires. Otherwise, they remain a concept in your mind, somewhat distorted from their reality. How many times have you truly wanted something, and when it arrived, it wasn't what you expected, and you felt disappointed? Or was it even better than you could have imagined and felt delighted? Either way it's okay, as you are learning what works for you.

Your creative soul has inspired you to rendezvous with these cards to discover and play with the creation process. Each time you work with this oracle, you enter a sacred gateway carved with the axiom 'Create Thyself'. As you step through this threshold, you will awaken new concepts about the creative universe and form stronger bonds with your soul.

Each card comprises a message and a Conscious Creator Masterclass. The message tells you what is significant in your life now and how that may unfold. The masterclass delves deeper into the card topic through visualisation, journal work, reflections, and actions. Think of these cards as a personal spiritual assistant, helping you fine-tune what you want.

THE LANGUAGE OF MANIFESTATION

The privilege of a lifetime is to become who you truly are.
—*Carl Jung*

When we learn a new language, we learn to combine words, sounds, gestures, and symbols that allow us to communicate in a specific community. The language of manifestation is an organised way to clarify the method of creating and attracting desired things and experiences.

Here are five steps to understand the language and process of manifestation.

1. Requesting Your Desire

Each day, you continually ask for things, even if you are unaware that you do. Throughout your daily life, you will experience likes and dislikes. The 'likes' encourage you to seek more of what brings you enjoyment, fostering similar experiences. The 'dislikes' will inspire new ideas to create better ones; for example, "I really don't like how that person spoke to me" can inspire a unique communication style with yourself and others. It is incredible what we can create from an uncomfortable situation. You begin to appreciate the contrast of life and how it helps to create bigger questions that, in turn, create bigger desires. If you experience something that hurts so much that you can't make sense of it, be inspired to seek help from a trusted loved one or professional to rebalance and heal.

2. The Universe Receives Your Request

The universe receives your request and builds it in the multidimensional, energetic realm. As soon as you send out your request, it is created. You may not be able to see it yet, but if you tune in to the feeling, you know it exists because you have instigated the request. You already understand that different vibrations evoke different emotions. You have felt positive or negative energy flow from someone even though you couldn't see it. You may have even felt the atmosphere of a fight or love when entering a room.

Just as you receive information about your feelings, so does the universe. What differs is the interpretation. The universe works from a loving standpoint. Love is unconditional, meaning it sees and experiences everything without judgement. You receive more of the energy you send out. It doesn't reward or take away.

3. Aligning with Your Desired Request

How will you transform to align your vibration with your desires? Alignment entails resonating at the same frequency or wavelength as what you want. You desire things, experiences, or changes because you believe they will make you feel better, more satisfied, or safer. Tune in to a desired sensation whenever you want — you know what the sensation feels like because you created it. Don't overthink it; alignment occurs naturally when you appreciate the process as you journey towards your desires. In other words, you find enjoyment in life's journey while progressing towards everything you desire. Thus, you are also aligned with your higher self, the wisdom of your soul.

If you encounter difficulties, worry, overwhelm, or anxiety, look away — remove your attention for a little while. Then, take some time to rebalance and realign yourself. Take another look at the challenges with the perspective of, "I will find a solution." This is a form of self-love.

Challenges will always be a part of the human experience. Returning to alignment provides enhanced access to your soul's wisdom. This enables you to strengthen your spiritual resilience, gracefully navigating life's fluctuations. As you embrace the insights gained from both ups and downs, your life's quality expands, igniting a desire for even greater aspirations. Embrace contrasting experiences to generate new wishes. This is a way to understand the creative process and why you feel negative emotions.

4. Clarifying Your Desired Request

You don't have to keep reminding the universe of your request — it has already got it. However, time allows you to expand or refine emotions, reactions, and thoughts about your request or replace it with a new request fashioned from the previous one. Imagine you are sculpting or crafting your desires into being, like a potter moulding clay.

5. Receiving Your Desired Request

You understand you are worthy and believe your request is possible. Aligned with the frequency of your desire, you open your heart to allow, catch, and receive desires, becoming what you desire.

This is learning the discipline to not resist your stream of wellbeing and desires. To allow and receive is your natural state of being, however, it is often buried by layers of justification, complaints, and blame that will cause you to argue for your limitations. Along life's journey, you may also have picked up and taken on board others' beliefs and ideas. Introspection, awareness, and a willingness to dissolve these layers will reveal the authentic you and a new-found trust, certainty, and confidence. You are transforming and levelling up.

When your requests arrive, they will inspire new desires to create. You then begin again at step one and request a new desire, and so on. The more you practise these five steps, the easier they will become, and eventually, the steps will disappear as you integrate the process, and it will just be how you live and create your life.

Unintentional Manifestations

While you have the power to create your reality, it's possible to manifest things you don't desire unintentionally. Our subconscious minds are often influenced by beliefs and conclusions accumulated throughout life. To introspectively examine these beliefs and thoughts, courage is needed to determine if they still serve us. It's important to acknowledge that your past beliefs have served a purpose, guiding you to this point in life. If it feels appropriate, express gratitude for their role and release them.

You can't create for others; likewise, others can't for you. However, you can rendezvous with experiences and others that resonate with similar vibrations. Knowing how you feel about something brings an understanding of the story attached to it, which you can then choose to adjust and transform.

Everything you desire has two aspects: the wanted and the not wanted. When you want more love, you know this because you have experienced a lack of love. We live in a world of duality, where seeing two sides of the same thing helps us measure and test its validity.

Here is an example of the process of an unintentional manifestation. The thought, "I want a day off", drops into your mind. Similar ideas come to join that idea, "I've been working hard; I'm allowed to take a day off." Your mind will sift through your memory and apply reasonable suggestions to justify the statement. It will then add reactive emotions to build importance until the 'day off' becomes necessary: "I need a day off. I'm a good person, and other people have days off. I need a day to catch up with myself so I don't get sick."

But what if your obligations don't leave room for a day off? Your mind begins to take this personally: "It's not fair; I work so hard." A feeling of powerlessness begins to creep in and erode your certainty and stability. The unrealised desire becomes an affirmation of inner disempowerment. Because of this insecurity, your mind begins to resonate with weakness, and your outside world begins to bring similar frequencies of experience. It may come in the form of a head cold, a flat battery, an unexpected deadline at work, or a bill to pay. You feel overwhelmed and victimised, and anger develops — it must be someone's fault because you wouldn't do this to yourself. The blame game begins. The dramatic feeling will be with you for hours or days, depending on how much attention you give to it. Eventually, your focus will shift or something will uplift you, and your reality will change to match your new predominate vibrations.

THE PATH OF MOST AND LEAST ALLOWANCE — RELEASING RESISTANCE

When you release resistance,
you become a magnet for greatness.
—*Gabby Bernstein*

In its simplest explanation, *allowance* is the ability to let everything be in each moment. You don't have to like it or tolerate it, but you don't try to run, assign blame, deny it, or push it away. Just let it be. Adjust your emotions and expectations, and adapt to a balanced perspective. *Resistance* is the inability to manage the reality of the moment. Imagine trying to drive your car with the handbrake on. The car still moves, but its performance is lacking. After a while, you can smell burning rubber tyres as the friction of the brake rubs against the moving tyre. You are still moving forwards, but the car must expend much more energy to get you anywhere, and it won't be a pleasant trip. This is resistance. Anytime you introduce doubt, fear, worry, or negative thoughts about a desired request, consciously or unconsciously, you put your handbrake on. This can lead to self-sabotage and justifying by arguing for limitations.

When you resist, your body becomes stiff, gripping and holding, not wanting to move. Or the opposite might occur, and you want to run and hide. Truths may be swirling, searching for a way to be heard and find balance, but fear stops them at your throat, and you swallow them down. You become reluctant to let go because hanging on to what you know feels safer, even if it is not what you desire. Your soul gently says, "Give it a go," but the fear about what you believe will happen screams a big "NO".

Working through this deck will provide the tools and confidence to gently release resistance one small step at a time.

The Path of Most Allowance or Least Resistance
Your higher self sees the larger picture and considers the 'path of most allowance' to your desire. This will include what you need to leave aside. Recognise any resistance as a signal from your higher self, prompting you to take action. When your soul's desires begin to rise into your awareness, remember what you are feeling. What fears and limiting beliefs are growing? This is a beautiful opportunity to understand your beliefs and why you're not taking action. You consciously want a better life, so what is holding you back?

As you navigate the path of most allowance, imagine it is a stream leading you to an ocean of infinite desires. Allowing yourself to be swept up will take you exactly where you need to be. Surrendering to your higher self doesn't mean losing control — you just let go of the things holding you away from your desires. Don't worry, you don't have to dive in all at once and hope for the best — just dip your toe in. Get used to the feeling, and then gently move into the stream, exhilarated that you are on the way. Enjoy the journey. When you are ready to let go, know the stream will lead you to pleasing, and sometimes astonishing, manifestations.

The Path of Least Allowance or Most Resistance
Are you ready for your desired change, relationship, or job? The desire may cause undue stress when you are unsure how it will emerge or if it will give you what you want. Maybe you want to be in a relationship but fear being hurt, or you want to work for

yourself but are unsure if you will be financially safe. Whenever you say, "I would really love this thing ..." it's already on its way. However, if you add, "... But I'm not sure how it will happen," you add resistance, and your desire falls further down the list of desires manifesting.

Imagine the same before-mentioned stream scenario. To create your desires through effort and resistance, you will take a boat into the stream for protection. You have been told it is an unsafe and challenging world. Because of a need to control, you will also need oars to move and steer. You will drag the boat to the water's edge, put it in the water, jump in and proceed to paddle against the current. In this scenario, you will eventually create a nearly slightly disappointing version of your desire. How often have you believed the path to anything must be hard to appreciate? This is only true if you think it is. If it feels right, be open to the path of least resistance or most allowance.

Managing Resistance

When deliberate actions build positive momentum, lasting change happens more organically. There will be days when your mind challenges the concepts in this deck and your new approach. When this happens, you can choose to respond in one of the following ways:

- Breathe deeply and meditate.
- Have a rest day to adjust and adapt to your new perceptions. Don't give it another thought — just begin again tomorrow.
- If you want to carry on, remember that when you push against resistance, it can push back even harder. Let it be there. Let it have its opinion and say to that part of yourself, "I respect and

honour your opinion; after all, it is a long-held belief that has become part of my everyday way of being. But just for today, I want to try something different."

You are at the beginning of a profound shift in your thinking. Be patient with yourself, as some beliefs are easier to let go of than others.

YOUR MANIFESTATION NAME

Just a tender sense of my own process, that holds something of my connection with the Divine.
—*Percy Bysshe Shelley*

Your manifestation name embodies the magical process of creating your reality. It opens your heart and mind to your soul's vision and wisdom about the creation process. It becomes a reference point, where all your dreams and desires accumulate. Using a name also makes it easier to recognise the feeling of your inner creator and have a conversation about manifesting. This will inspire you to put processes and systems in place to follow the path of joyous creating, instead of fearful responding. The meditation in Card One, *Manifestation Name*, will help you discover what to call the part of your being that deals with acts of manifestation. Use this name in the visualisation exercises for the following cards to support your desired manifestations. Your 'manifesting spirit' is the part of you that is now named. If your manifestation name hasn't arrived before you do the visualisations, a substitute word is provided to use instead.

My Manifestation Name

My manifestation name is Asherah. She is an ancient sacred moon-tree goddess whose fruit was said to bring gifts of inspiration and wisdom. She has faded from the physical world, but her energy still weaves through the Tree of Life. Her essence is at the heart of teachings that assist us in bringing Spirit into the physical so that we can experience the expansion of our soul through our physical bodies. She first entered my meditations about twenty years ago as a violet seed. I was encouraged to plant the seed in my heart. It became a part of my inner technology that would grow as my awareness expanded into the idea that life happens from me, not to me.

Her message to me:

A liquid point of light flows within your essence; this is the beginning of all creation. Just by reading this, you will feel it stir and seed your dreams, and every time you have a new vision or passion, it flows to this seed. As you plant this seed within your heart, it is simultaneously planted into the heart of Mother Earth and Father Sky; all are connected and conspire to bring your dreams and desires to life. Your job is to relax, knowing that your tree is growing and will soon bear fruit; all is coming. Live each day as if all your dreams and desires are here, and one day soon, they will be. You are loved, and you are worthy.

CONSCIOUS CREATION MASTERCLASS

How to Use the Cards for Conscious Creation Mastery

The cards have been designed to empower the possibility that you create your life. As well as being an oracle, the 'Message' section introduces the concepts of each card. The 'Conscious Creator Masterclass' section delves into how to work with, integrate, and apply the ideas in your manifestation practice.

To use the deck for the Conscious Creator Masterclass, begin with Card One and work through each of the 45 cards sequentially. Once you have completed the course, you can randomly choose a card whenever you want to delve deeper and work with the information for self-inquiry. The information may be the same, but you are meeting it from a higher vibration and will experience expanded wisdom.

You can choose a card as often as you like, but I suggest you complete all the sections before moving on to another card to integrate the information into your daily life. Information never teaches. It remains a concept until it is embodied. Once experienced, you will begin to feel and understand it throughout your body, and you can decide whether to adopt the material or let it go.

The Three Sections of the Conscious Creation Masterclass

Visualisation
The visualisations serve as guided meditations intended to merge the theme of each card with your imagination, allowing you to

immerse yourself in the imagery and concepts within your inner world. As you feel the emotions and intuitive awareness within yourself, you tune in to your soul's wisdom. Your whole being resonates with the possibility that this thing you desire is possible. It is also a way to connect with and understand the topic of the card more deeply.

You will be asked to place the card at your feet, whether lying, sitting, or standing, to ground the frequency of the card's topic. Imagine planting a seed that will help you grow and reach the highest potential of your desires.

The visualisations are written in the present, so you can experience the creative wisdom of your inner creator each time you encounter them.

The visualisations call to close your eyes. Obviously, you can't read the exercise with your eyes closed. You have the option of reading it or recording it. Both ways will help you understand and integrate the information. Closing my eyes makes it easier to let go of the outside world and enter my inner world. We are all different, and if you can activate your inner world with your eyes open or focus on an object or candle flame, there is no need to close your eyes during the visualisations.

I suggest you record the meditations on your smartphone, tablet, or computer with your voice, then close your eyes while listening to the playback. Your voice is unique to you and activates deeper understandings from your soul.

You may also like to play gentle music or burn incense or aromatherapy oils.

Journal Work

The questions in this section clarify your unique perspective on the card's topic. Writing or drawing what you experience gives the ideas swirling in your head a place to land. When your thoughts become anchored in the outside world, you can see them with a clarity that is obscured when they are too close and in your head. Harness your unique viewpoint to choose what to keep and what to leave on the path.

Many beautiful journals are available for purchase, but you can also use your computer, other electronic devices, or an exercise book. Allow your inspiration to choose. A journal is an invaluable record of your creative experiences and will serve as a reference for the future.

Reflections and Actions

This section will help bring the card's theme to life. The reflections enhance an understanding of the theme, while the actions help you experience it. Before you read or act, take a deep breath in and out, then open yourself to trying something new. I recommend you attempt each suggestion at least once to see what happens. Think of this as a manifesting experiment.

USING THE CARDS AS AN ORACLE

Truth is always present; it only needs to lift the iron lids of the mind's eye to read its oracles.
—Ralph Waldo Emerson

The Welcome
This deck has found its way into your life because you are ready to feel, hear, and see the messages within. Welcome your deck by holding it to your heart. Feel the energy flow from the cards into your heart, illuminating your creative, intuitive powers.

Preparing to Give a Reading
The calmer and more balanced you are when doing inner work, the more precise your answers will be. A receptive heart and mind will help you let go of issues, worries, or problems for the duration of the reading. This meditative state will help you greet your creative soul in a balanced, non-judgemental and loving way. Be present. Allow everything to be as it is, uninfluenced by the past or the future.

The Intention
Before each reading, establish your intention with an invocation or meditation. This invites the presence of your angels, guides or light beings and connects you to the wisdom of your heart.

Sit quietly with your cards in your hands and close your eyes. Breathe gently and imagine the creative white light of the universe flowing into the room, swirling all around you. Breathe in the light, knowing it is filled with unconditional love and healing. This illuminates a small golden light in your heart centre. This is your light of awareness, a guiding presence full of warmth and joy. As you rest in the love and wisdom of your sacred light, gently open your eyes. You are now ready to start your reading.

The Question

If you don't have a question, be open to the information that comes. The Law of Attraction will bring information that resonates with the themes and predominant energies radiating from you, which will always be for your highest growth with love.

If you have a question, phrase it so it requires more than a 'yes' or 'no' answer. Ask yourself what it is you want to know. For example, "Will I get this job?" might become, "What are the opportunities and challenges of accepting this job?" Whether you and your partner will get married might be posed as, "How will my relationship with [name] progress over the next two years?" Be specific and use names and time frames where applicable. Adding more information and reframing the question opens the reading to more possibilities.

The Shuffle

Pick up your deck. If you have a question, hold it in your mind as you handle the cards. Shuffle or rearrange them in a way that is easy for you. You may like to cut the deck if this feels right. You can take the cards from the top or fan them out and choose from anywhere in the deck. The more you play with your cards, the sooner you will find the best way for you. Remember, there is no right or wrong way to do this.

Jumping Cards

A jumping card is one that falls or 'jumps' out of the deck as you shuffle. Take note of these — they offer a magical insight into what you felt or understood at the time when they jumped.

Reversed Cards

When a card is dealt upside down, it can be read as reversed. Some readers attach importance to reversed cards, and some don't. There are no rules here. As always, do what feels best for you. In my experience, a reversed card may signify delays and obstacles or that more information is to come.

The Future

Our lives exist in the present, with the future unfolding one moment at a time. The cards will show what *could* happen based on your present circumstances as well as giving you any action you can take now to manifest your desires.

Training Your Intuition

Each time you choose a card or lay out a spread, place the images face up. Look at the images one at a time, close your eyes and imagine yourself in each picture. What do you feel? What sensations, words, or images come to you? Write down everything. Spend thirty seconds to a minute doing this, and then look up the card's meaning in the guidebook.

MANIFESTATION SPREADS

When we lay cards out in a set pattern, it is called a spread. Consider each card's message in combination with the cards around it. This allows different pathways and perspectives to be introduced to the reading.

These spreads have been designed for this deck to offer clarity and healing in your readings. Please feel free to also use your favourite spreads.

Actively Experiencing the Spreads

A different way to play with the cards is to lay them out on the floor, with at least 30 cm or a foot between the cards. Use one of the card spreads below or any of your favourite layouts. Stand before the card spread and imagine the cards want to converse with you.

Stand in the position of the first card, pick it up and ask it these questions:

- What do you want me to feel?
- What do you want me to see?

Put it back on the floor, close your eyes, and engage all your senses to embody the answers. Associate yourself into the picture. Then, ask, "Do you have any other information for me?" You're invited to ask any other questions that come to you. Take as long as you need, then open your eyes. Put the card back on the floor and repeat for the other cards in the spread.

Have fun!

The Oracle of Creation: Single-Card Spread

This card represents something extraordinary you need to recognise in your manifesting practice.

Shuffle the deck (close your eyes while you do this if you like). Fan out the deck and choose one card with any hand. Look at the card's image for a while, then close your eyes and picture the image in your mind's eye. Allow yourself to relax in the knowledge you are opening to deep, inner wisdom about the creation process. After a while, you will move beyond the image into your inner world of creation. As you do this, allow thoughts, feelings, words, or images to arise in your mind spontaneously. This is your soul's wisdom being made apparent to you. Don't react to these; simply witness them. You can reflect on what you sense afterwards, integrating it into your practice and the reading.

When you feel ready, bring your focus back to the card image, and breathe it in and out. Open your eyes and read the message.

Soul Desire Message: Two-Card Spread

This small but insightful spread helps you understand why you want or need a specific desire and any resistance you hold about it.

Card 1: Now — What is holding you back from your desires?
Card 2: Message — What do your desires want to tell you?

Creative Vision: Four-Card Spread

Use this spread to inspire creative thinking at the beginning of a project, or anytime you are overthinking. It will expand your insight by bringing a different perspective and laying out inspired actions to help you attract your desires.

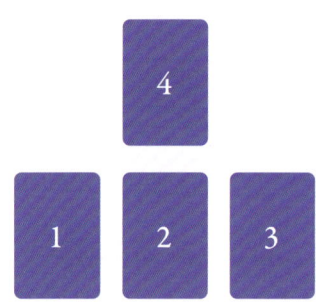

Card 1: Now — What desires are most prominent in your thoughts?
Card 2: Past — What experiences from the recent past prompted these desires?
Card 3: Future — How or where will your desires appear?
Card 4: Opportunity — Any action to take.

Creative Healing: Four-Card Spread

Here is a short but powerful spread to heal whatever holds you back from your dreams and desires.

Card 1: Now — The beliefs most dominant in your thinking.

Card 2: Love — Something that makes your heart smile, your soul desires.

Card 3: Fear — Something that makes your heart sink, your false desires.

Card 4: Heal — Action you can take to change any outdated beliefs holding you back from your dreams and desires.

CARD MEANINGS

and Conscious Creator Masterclasses

I. Manifestation Name

Discover and co-create with your inner creator.

Your questions about manifesting desires have opened a direct connection to your soul wisdom. It will come as a name, flowing into your awareness with a fresh approach to creating a unique, dream life.

Message

Your manifestation name is developing and will soon open a direct link to the principles of creation. You are unlocking a new understanding of yourself and how to design your life. Your name becomes a conduit for all your guides, angels, loved ones, and light beings to stream their love and messages to you.

If your name has already manifested, breathe life into it and allow it to expand into its role as a guide. Keep your name as long as it inspires and feels good. When it no longer does either, a new name will emerge with a deeper understanding of creation.

Your manifestation name activates and helps you embody your inner creator. It lets you easily recognise this part of you by how it feels. It opens a dialogue about crafting your life and how it happens in two ways: unconsciously (not aware) and consciously (aware). You can't get this wrong. Any problematic situation allows you to learn, heal, and grow. Each moment is an opportunity for you to learn more about yourself. When you ask questions, new perceptions and skills flow into your mind and body that spark new quests to begin and unfold.

Explore the exercises in the masterclass to embody the message and discover the name of your manifesting spirit.

Conscious Creator Masterclass: Discover Your Manifestation Name

Open yourself to receiving your manifestation name. It will form in the coming days and weeks if it doesn't come today. If your name has already manifested, be open to an expansion or change of your name.

Visualisation

Place the *Manifestation Name* card at your feet. Gently close your eyes. Sense your body and concentrate on your breathing. Follow your breath inward. Hold for five seconds. Breathe out and release all tension. Relax. Then, focus on the middle of your chest. Sense your breathing moving in and out of your heart.

Imagine you ride a wave of light deep into your heart. Riding the wave like an expert surfer, you are taken to a clear crystal door inscribed with letters that seem to form a name. If you have done this before, your manifestation name will appear.

Your willingness to be a conscious creator opens the door. You step through onto a large, circular, revolving platform. All around you, light rays filled with your questions and desires come and go. The display is beautiful. You are watching your questions and desires move outward into the universe and realise that your answers and manifestations are forming.

A profound silence then descends around you and opens a portal, allowing for your manifestation name to flow to you. If you already have your name, deeper truths will flow. Open your heart to receive this information. Stay here for as long as you like — at least thirty seconds.

When you are ready, the portal gently fades away, and the rays of creation swirl again. You step out of the light rays and remember this feeling of endless possibilities as you float through the door. Notice the name on the door as it may have changed. Focus on your breath and let it guide you back to your physical self. Open your eyes and smile.

Journal Work
When you have finished the visualisation, say out loud the name/s or word/s that came to you. Then, write or draw two thoughts or ideas this name or names invoke in you. This process helps to melt away doubt while fully restoring belief in your ability to create your manifestations.

Reflections and Actions
If your manifestation name/s hasn't come to you yet, use a word that represents joy.

To help you find it, you can also research your first or middle name. Every name has a meaning and can give you more information to add to your manifestations. For example, 'Denise' means "devoted to Dionysus", the Greek god of wine, fertility, and ecstasy. My conclusion is to make the process of creation joyous and fun for myself and others.

When you find a name or names, try them on to see how they feel. Say out loud, "My manifestation name is _____." It might feel weird initially but keep going; you are creating a belief in yourself. You will know a name is right for you when you sense a quiet recognition or knowing.

Your soul is infinite and knows you can create what you desire. If you want something but don't feel worthy or are unsure how it will arrive, hand over your dreams and desires to your inner creator. Say, "[Manifestation name], I would love _____. I open my heart to receive it. Thank you."

2. Waking Up

Discover and create from your authentic soul self.

Your dreams and desires continually push against outdated or limiting beliefs as they search for a way to manifest in your life. You will feel this as an urge to live an authentic, soul-inspired life.

Message

Triggered by a deep yearning to live a genuine, fulfilling, and inspiring life, authentic soul qualities are entering your awareness. They may come as a sudden burst of insight or information that builds upon previous discoveries. You are awakening into the same world but seeing it through new eyes that recognise the path towards genuine and pleasing life encounters.

Invite your curiosity to rouse fresh perspectives and possibilities for you to experience. The star on the card depicts two triangles merging. The downwards-pointing triangle symbolises the divine feminine principle of infinite possibilities and dream inspiration, while the upwards-pointing triangle represents the masculine principle of thoughtful action and expression of desire.

The heart is a combination of both radiating outward through the colours of gold (wisdom), red/pink (love), and blue (honesty), which creates authentic, practical insights for you to apply in your daily life.

The more you recognise your true qualities, the greater your inner light shines upon solutions. You are doing so well; you can't get this process wrong. Your life will continually bring opportunities for you to awaken into greater awareness. Relax and enjoy this time of authentic desires moving into your world.

Explore the exercises in the masterclass to embody the message and gently awaken your authenticity.

Conscious Creator Masterclass: Self-Inquiry for Awakening

The previous masterclass introduced your manifestation name. This masterclass helps you understand your authentic self as you discover the mystery of awakening.

Visualisation

Place the *Waking Up* card at your feet. In your mind, repeat your manifestation name or the word 'awaken' nine times. Gently close your eyes. Feel your body and concentrate on your breathing. Follow your breath inward. Hold for five seconds. Breathe out and release all tension. Relax and breathe naturally.

A bright light from your soul surrounds you. Breathe the light of your soul into your heart. Your heart opens so wide you can walk into it. Here, you stand in a space where you are free to be you. Not who you think you must be, but the private you: full of dreams, hopes, and desires. Familiarise yourself with this place. Adjust your energy to honour this loving space. There is no judgement here, just a limitless quantum field of possibilities.

In this place, become self-aware by getting to know yourself.

Ask yourself some questions. Allow any thoughts, sensations, colours, or feelings to come to you spontaneously.

- Who am I? (Stay here for one minute and quietly listen.)
- What is my deepest desire? What do I truly want? (Stay here for one minute and quietly listen.)
- What is my purpose? What do I want to contribute to the world? (Stay here for one minute and quietly listen.)
- What am I grateful for? What do I love in my life now? (Stay here for one minute and quietly listen.)

Breathe more light into your heart and imagine your heart expanding even more. Love, knowingness, and bliss fill your heart. Each heartbeat pulses golden light through you, filling the room with golden light. Allow golden light to melt away anything that holds you away from your dreams. Let it melt away any masks you wear and allow yourself to shine.

Now, as you breathe, bring your heart closer and closer to you. Call your energy back until it is contained within your body. Your best life is yet to come because you are transcending into your soul's vision. Be here now. Wiggle your toes and fingers. Stretch your body and open your eyes.

Journal Work

Write or draw any answers you received to the questions you asked yourself in the visualisation.

- Who am I?
- What is my deepest desire? What do I truly want?
- What is my purpose? What do I want to contribute to the world?
- What am I grateful for? What do I love in my life now?

Reflections and Actions: Clarification

New experiences and information clarify how you want to live and create. Lives can be busy, and often, information slips behind your awareness. But don't worry, any information needed will awaken into your awareness when you are ready to receive it. Over time, your authentic self becomes more precise and louder. Your awareness expands to allow more of your authentic self to point you towards possibilities beyond any limitations.

Repeat the visualisation monthly around the time of the new moon, then look over your previous journal work answers. Consider what you have written or drawn and decide if it is still relevant. Then, write or draw anything you want to add. If something no longer feels relevant, remove it, cross it out, or draw over it.

At any time, ask your manifesting name to make clear the desires of your authentic self. An answer will come in the following 24 hours.

3. BELIEFS

Opinions and conclusions filtering your experience.

The longer you ruminate on specific thoughts about a subject, the more you allow these thoughts to form into a belief pattern that filters out what desires you can or can't experience.

Message

Your beliefs are challenged to help you realise if they connect with your values. Do you *believe* your beliefs? Are they helping or hindering your journey of life? Beliefs are helpful if they move you towards knowing. Knowing is the integration of belief into certainty. If you are arguing a point, it is likely against another's belief that does not align with your values. When you know, you know — whatever another thinks won't sway your conviction of certainty.

A belief begins with a single thought. The longer you dwell on that thought, the greater its influence becomes. If you keep going, it will become a habit of thought that forms a belief. It then becomes entangled with your everyday way of living, where it gains certainty. In the future when this belief activates, it feels familiar, so you believe it to be correct and therefore will keep you safe.

If your life is pleasing, keep practising your beliefs. They are a springboard for more enjoyable experiences and a journey towards knowing and self-realisation. If your life is unacceptable, use this experience to point you towards new thoughts. This will allow new beliefs to form that feel more authentic. It's easier to identify what you like when you know what you don't like. You can dissolve an outdated belief by thinking of a new thought that feels better.

The card image depicts the many perspectives and thoughts of our world. If you rise to the light hovering over the earth, you will appreciate a bigger picture of different beliefs. You don't have to believe these perceptions. However, you have the inherent right to discover what beliefs are true for you and allow everyone else to live theirs. Think of yourself as a thought pioneer, preparing for a new interpretation of reality and knowing.

Explore the exercises in the masterclass to embody the message and discover what beliefs feel true for you.

Conscious Creator Masterclass: Lovingly Examining Beliefs for Relevance and Truth

---

The previous masterclass awakened your authenticity and new possibilities. This masterclass helps you sift through possible beliefs to sense if they are authentic to you.

Visualisation

Place the *Beliefs* card at your feet. Gaze softly at the image. In your mind, repeat your manifestation name or the word 'truth' nine times. Gently close your eyes. Tilt your head upwards slightly and focus on the place between your eyebrows. Take four deep, slow breaths. Imagine a door into your mind coming into focus. It opens and invites you in. You float effortlessly into your brilliant mind. All around you are small, radiant, coloured balls connected by streaks of lightning. Each coloured ball contains a different belief. Your inner mindscape is breathtakingly beautiful.

As your inner eye and senses adjust, you tune in to the unique frequencies emanating from the balls, which match the colours and beliefs they contain. Your attention is drawn to one ball; as you focus on it, it becomes brighter and bigger, and the outside becomes transparent. Take a look — what do you see? Then, like magic, you realise you can float into the ball. Inside, sense and see how your life could be through the perception of this belief. Play in this space for at least thirty seconds and take note of feelings, colours, symbols, or words you encounter. You can explore another ball or come back another time to investigate other beliefs.

When ready, draw your awareness from the ball and gently float towards the doorway. Bring with you the findings and colour/s of your ball/s. Place the colour/s around your body to create a magnetic field that resonates with your authenticity. Glide into your outer world. Breathe your colour/s in and out and slowly open your eyes. Re-orient your body and mind by focusing on the *Beliefs* card. Imagine infinite possibilities are all around you. You are much more than you believe you are.

Journal Work

This journal work will create stepping stones into your inner truth, leading to greater understanding of your beliefs.

- Write or draw about the feelings, colours, symbols, or words you encountered in the visualisation.
- Write or draw about any 'belief balls' you experienced during the visualisation. Did you recognise the belief? Is the belief true for you?
- Write or draw about how one new belief would benefit your life.

Reflections and Actions

These exercises help reveal any original purposes or situations that created your beliefs, and you can formulate new ideas and beliefs more aligned with your truth.

Try not complaining for 24 hours. If you do, gently ask yourself, "Why am I complaining, and what belief is it serving?" Complaining feeds beliefs about being a victim. Sometimes, it is easier to justify our experiences instead of using them to create a new belief. Someone or something familiar often feels easier and less risky than change, even if it brings a result that isn't ideal.

Try this: With a trusted companion, one at a time, wear a blindfold and assign a simple task for each other to do in the house. Look after each other. When you have both had a turn, discuss what other senses took over and if your beliefs about how you gather outside information helped or hindered. For example, a common belief is "I need to see it to believe it is real." But is something any less real if you can't see it?

4. GRATITUDE

Appreciation multiplies blessings.

Gratitude is a conditional emotion expressed when something good has happened or arrived. Imagine what you can manifest through unconditional gratitude, purely for the joy of appreciating.

Message

Look around and name one thing you are grateful for. Congratulations, you have just raised your vibration and opened a pathway for desires to enter your life effortlessly. When you direct your attention towards appreciation, your heart and mind harmonise, you dissolve stress, and cultivate greater joy and hope.

Gratitude soothes your nervous system and releases the feel-good neurotransmitters dopamine and serotonin from your brain. Heightened feelings of safety and abundance will follow. Even in difficult times, you can discover things to be grateful for: a beautiful sunset, a smile from a stranger, a phone call or virtual hug from a loved one, trees that give us oxygen, or the ability to choose.

Being grateful reveals a rich tapestry of life waiting to be seen and appreciated. Be like the person in the card's image who appreciates the fullness of life signified by the *taijitu*: the receptive *yin* embracing the creative *yang*. A dot of each exists in the other to remind us that each side carries the essence of the other. Appreciating all perspectives of life allows you to gracefully dance with the ebb and flow of life, just like the curves of the symbol.

Explore the exercises in the masterclass to embody the message and discover the wonderment of being grateful.

Conscious Creator Masterclass: Experience Gratitude

The previous masterclass informed you of your beliefs and whether they help or hinder your desires becoming manifest. This masterclass reveals new and different aspects of your life to be grateful for. Feeling a fullness of gratitude brings more things into your life to be thankful for.

Visualisation

Find a comfortable place to sit down. Place the *Gratitude* card at your feet. In your mind, repeat your manifestation name or the word 'grateful' nine times. Gently close your eyes. Sense your body and concentrate on your breathing. Take your focus to the middle of your chest. Breathe into your chest and notice tiny points of light. The points of light become swirling shades of blue and purple. They are brilliant lights of your soul that cultivate love, joy, and gratitude.

The room fills with blue and purple. It moves all around you, flowing over you in waves. Allow yourself to feel the wonderment of your soul's bliss. The room fills with blue and purple, representing the authentic bliss of your soul. These colours move around you, flowing over you in gentle waves. Allow yourself to feel the wonderment of your soul's ecstasy.

A glowing *taijitu* emerges from the blue and purple. Visualise holding it between your hands like the image. As you touch the sphere, in your mind's eye, you can see people streaming by. You realise they are people from your life, past and present. You can intuitively understand why they are or have been in your life, as well as the creations that have emerged from past experiences or are now emerging from recent physical or envisioned interactions.

Take your time and allow this information to flow into your being. You are opening to a deeper understanding and the joy of co-creation. We are all brothers and sisters walking each other home. Stay here for as long as you need.

Breathe in the blue and purple. Imagine it flows through you and out the bottom of your feet into the earth for the healing and gratitude of Mother Earth. She thanks you and reminds you: As you heal and appreciate yourself, you also help all living beings heal and appreciate themselves. You are love, and you are loved.

Take a deep breath and feel yourself returning to your physical body and life. As you are floating back, fill your body with gratitude and appreciation. Wiggle your toes and fingers, stretch your body, and open your eyes.

Journal Work

Write or draw a story about a person from your visualisation who positively impacted your life. Then, write or draw about what you learnt about yourself from this relationship. Name one thing about meeting this person that you are grateful for.

Write or draw a story about a person from your visualisation who had a negative impact on your life. Then, write or draw about what you learnt about yourself from this relationship. Name one thing about meeting this person that you are grateful for.

Reflections and Actions

Ask to find the blessings in any experience. Write two things you are grateful for on separate pieces of paper. Ask a friend or family member to do the same. Arrange a time to get together. Put all the gratitude slips in one jar and take turns choosing a piece of paper. Read what it says aloud and ask the writer to share their feelings about gratitude.

As soon as you wake up in the morning, bring to your mind at least one thing you are joyously grateful for. Then, take that feeling as far into your day as you can. To begin with, you may only get as far as the shower or breakfast. As you practice, this joyous gratitude will flow further into your day. If it falls away, you will be aware enough to refocus.

When someone compliments you, receive it with grace and gratitude by saying, "Thank you." Many of us are more comfortable giving, but if no one received, we wouldn't have anyone to give to! It may have taken great courage to compliment you, so don't diminish their feelings by dismissing, belittling, or making an excuse because you may be embarrassed. Thank them, be grateful, and more things to be thankful for will come to you.

Anything you can't be grateful for is baggage and will deplete your energy. Anything that you can be thankful for is fuel that will increase your energy.

5. WELLBEING

Create a desire for vitality.

Your body translates your thoughts into chemistry that affects your wellbeing, caring for you without judgment. Foster alignment and greater wellbeing by accepting and loving your body.

Message

Your body is about to feel more at ease. You'll find it easier to cultivate gentle, loving thoughts and vibrations about your health that will influence your body's chemistry in ways that enhance your overall sense of wellbeing. Accompanying you everywhere, your body cares for you without judgement. As the caretaker of your body, everything you consume, whether food or information, creates an inner environment that makes your heart sing or shrink. To offer your body a more balanced perspective and vibrational alignment, consider saying:

I accept you as you are. Thank you for being my soul's vehicle. I love the sensations you offer that alert me to adjust something or seek a health practitioner. You are important, and together, we can manifest greater wellbeing.

Imagine the layers of the sacred heart in the image are your mind, body, and soul in union. When all these aspects agree—also known as alignment or vibrational balance—there is no resistance to a beautiful, pleasurable sense of self. The waves are different qualities of light and love that flow into every cell in your body. They revitalise, harmonise, and love you. Let all be as it is. All is well.

Celebrate this flourishing relationship with yourself. It is the most important relationship you will ever experience, and every other relationship reflects this.

To gain a greater sense and understanding about wellbeing, explore the following masterclass.

Conscious Creator Masterclass: Generating Wellness

The previous masterclass taught you the importance of gratitude and counting your blessings in manifesting. This masterclass softens, soothes, and harmonises your relationship with your body.

Visualisation
Place your hands on your lap with the *Wellbeing* card at your feet. In your mind, repeat your manifestation name or the word 'well' nine times. Gently close your eyes. Sense your body and concentrate on your breathing. Follow your breath inward. Hold

for five seconds. Breathe out and release all tension. Relax and breathe naturally.

In your mind's eye, imagine you are standing on a beach on a beautiful tropical island. The sun, perched high in the sky, shines its warming, healing rays upon you. The rays transform into a soothing, liquid gold as they touch you.

Take off your shoes and move down to the clear, turquoise-blue water. Step into the water, look out at the horizon, and allow your body to communicate a hurt that has become embedded in your body. You see a hammock strung up between two palm trees and feel the urge to climb into it. You instantly melt into it. Warm, golden light flows over you, bathing you with remarkable healing properties.

Relax into your natural vitality and scan your body from head to toe. Then, settle your attention on your sacred heart and imagine you receive a message from your soul through your body. It may be a symbol, words, colours, or a song; whatever comes shifts your attention and vibrations into a sense of love and wellness. Use your message to focus on your health for ten seconds. You will stop feeding discomfort for these ten seconds. Repeat in ten-second increments. As you focus on your message of harmony, you begin to nurture yourself.

A gentle sea breeze rocks the hammock from side to side. Any hurts start to loosen, untangle and leave your body on waves of golden, healing light. Stay here for at least one minute.

When ready, breathe that sense of thriving in and out. Each breath gently brings you into union with the beauty of your physical body. Allow the golden light of healing to stay with you for as long as you like. Take two deep breaths in and out. Wiggle your toes and fingers, stretch your body, open your eyes, and smile.

Journal Work

After finishing the visualisation, write or draw any messages you received from your sacred heart. Then, write or draw what wellbeing feels like in your body. Committing your notes and ideas to paper or a device is grounding them into this reality. It is planting a seed that can manifest in your physical body so you can get out of your head and into your life.

Reflections and Actions

If there is an aspect of your body you are not enjoying, enter into a conversation with it. Imagine it is sitting opposite you as a person or something you can easily communicate with. Ask what it needs from you and be open to listening with love.

By being present and honouring your body, you are open to wellbeing actions in all areas of your life. They will feel like logical next steps. It may mean adding more vegetables to your diet, making amends with a loved one, or seeking a health professional. Inner guidance is unique and differs for everyone.

Move your body, walk for half an hour daily, or try a yoga, dance, martial arts, or a gym class. Or put on your favourite music and ecstatically dance around your house for 10 minutes.

6. DESIRE

The path of most allowance.

The contradictions of life invoke clarity of your desires. Sensing a desire tells you it exists. Feel the joy of your desire now, opening a synchronistic path for its manifestation.

Message

You are the source of your desires, and they create your life experiences. At the heart of every desire is the longing to feel good and the ability to shape your life. The inner world of your soul is full of accumulated urges, spoken or unspoken, from this lifetime and many others waiting to be expressed in the physical. New 'wants' join this place every day, arising from the contrasting events and experiences you encounter. For example, someone being rude might bring the yearning to be around nicer people.

A desire comes into being when a thought or event creates a reaction that produces hormones which you feel as an emotion that, in turn, sparks a passion for something. Your whole body vibrates with the frequency of it. Tune in to that sensation and recall it often to make it tangible. Write about it in your journal to support the process and meditate on the feeling.

Your desires want to manifest fully like the rose in the image — to grow and expand into the infinite space of the universe. They wish to bring to life every nuance of your soul's dreams through unfurling every petal. When your desires arrive physically, you feel thrilled and satisfied. This leads to new perspectives that will incite more pathways to explore. The events and experiences of your life will grow in meaning as you experience what manifests.

Explore the exercises in the masterclass to embody the message and become the spark for greater desires.

Conscious Creator Masterclass: Feeling into a Desire

The previous masterclass made you aware that feeling a sense of wellbeing opens a flow of greater vitality to manifest throughout your body. This masterclass assists you to understand and clarify your desires.

Visualisation

Find a comfortable place to sit down. Place the *Desire* card at your feet. In your mind, repeat your manifestation name or the word 'desire' nine times. Gently close your eyes. Sense your body and concentrate on your breathing.

Take your focus to the middle of your chest. Passionate pulsations move within your heart. Your desires are gaining momentum, and you are ready to liberate them. Relax, all is well.

You have something unique to share with yourself and the world — authentic, untethered dreams and desires.

Bring one desire to mind. Then direct it to your heart centre. The seed of your desire has become a rosebud. Feel the passion of your desire and watch as your rosebud opens. As each petal unfolds, the elements of your desire are released as aromas. Imagine every cell in your body being filled with this unique perfume. Be the embodiment of your desire, letting it radiate like a sweet fragrance, attracting the elements and inspired actions needed for manifestation. Love every part of this process.

Stay in the fullness of your desire for at least a minute. Be your desire.

When you feel ready, focus on your breath. Even as you gently slide into your physicality, your desire is not yet set in stone. Time gives you space between your manifestations, so you have time to clarify your desire. You may add to it or go in a different direction. Just enter the feeling of your desire, and you will know. If clarity isn't coming, bask in the delight of already manifested dreams and desires.

Focus on your breath. Wiggle your toes and fingers. Then, stretch your body, and open your eyes.

Journal Work

After you have finished the visualisation, write or draw about the desire you liberated. Picture it in your mind. What does it look like? How do you feel when you are living it? And what new desires are being inspired by this experience?

Reflections and Actions

Keep your desires to yourself until you are sure they are for you. Don't let others, even well-meaning ones, talk you out of something because they can't see how it could happen.

Begin every day intending to feel your desires; for example, if you want more love, be love and give love. If you want nicer people in your life, be nicer to yourself and others.

A Desire Experiment

The following will activate your imagination and soul's truth.

Set aside at least half an hour each day to do only what you desire. When the time arrives, ask yourself, "What do I want to do right now? What comes to my mind that sounds good to me?"

Your mind will likely feel stressed, telling you all sorts of things you should do. Gently remind your consciousness that you are conducting an experiment and all is well. Then ask, "What do I want to do right now? What comes to mind that sounds good to me?"

As different ideas arise, let the one that most generates excitement motivate you. This idea will rise above the rest and spur you into action. It will be the next obvious step to take.

When this happens, do it — regardless of how silly or unproductive it seems. If it's something you can't do right now, write it in your journal and plan to do it later. Then ask, "What else do I want to do right now?" Have fun!

7. HEARTFULNESS

Manifest a heartfelt approach to life.

Heartfulness is an unconditional response to life, a gentle yet soul-affirming approach that prioritises what serves you in any situation, while allowing everything else to coexist.

Message

Whatever and however you are feeling today, your heart loves you unconditionally. Isn't it wonderful to know that you are always loved? Your heart radiates the expression of your soul's vision as impulses and inspirations you feel as aspects of love: bliss, joy, appreciation, empowerment, relief, and freedom.

Even if you have placed a shield around your heart, your soul's desires will find any cracks of allowance to flow through. They will turn up in your day and night dreams when your mind is quiet, or you feel loved. A broken heart opens the floodgates for your soul desires and the essence of you to arrive all at once. This is why a broken heart feels so raw and overwhelming.

You can become a cooperative component of your heart by developing mindfulness. Mindfulness is sitting in a quiet, present contemplation space, allowing thoughts and feelings to rise and fall without attachment. When you are present with your mind and body, you gain control of your emotions and thoughts and the shield or any hard edges around your heart begin to dissolve.

The card's image fills with soft colours that emanate distinct qualities of your soul's vision through your heart. Pink brings unconditional love. Purple transforms anything into higher vibrations. Blue communicates your authenticity. Gold activates sacred wisdom. In the middle of the heart is a pale *sri yantra*. A *yantra* is used as a point of focus during meditation and reflection. '*Sri*' loosely means 'respect, grace, or light'. It contains nine interlocking triangles — five pointing downwards, embodying the divine feminine of infinite possibilities and dream inspiration, and four pointing upwards, embodying the divine masculine of thoughtful action and desire expression. Concentrating on the place in the middle of the triangles draws the mind and heart into balance.

Explore the exercises in the masterclass to embody the message and become a magnet that draws heartfulness towards you.

Conscious Creator Masterclass: Giving and Receiving Love

The previous masterclass taught you that desires are expressions of your soul wanting to experience the physical. This masterclass opens and expands your heart's capacity for giving and receiving.

Visualisation

Before you begin the visualisation, try this mindfulness exercise that you can do anywhere, anytime, to dissolve stress and be present now. The present moment is where you feel most empowered and is the foundation for your future.

> Sit quietly and close your eyes. Imagine you draw a square in your mind's eye. Beginning at a corner at the top of your square, trace the line around the square as you breathe in for a count of four, hold for a count of four, breathe out for a count of four, and hold for a count of four. Once you have completed one round of the square, repeat three more times for four rounds, then open your eyes.

Find a comfortable place to sit or lie down. Place the *Heartfulness* card at your feet. In your mind, repeat your manifestation name or the word 'heart' nine times. Close your eyes and take four deep breaths. Breathe fully and deeply. Place a hand on your sacred heart centre in the middle of your chest and shift all your attention to this place. Imagine it to be a point of non-resistance, a soft spot that accepts everything as it is. Feel how easy it is to be here.

Imagine a sphere of rose quartz crystal floating and rotating above you. Waves of soft pink light filled with ease, acceptance, and forgiveness fill the room and swirl around you. The soft pink light draws you closer to your sacred heart.

As pink light washes over you, your heart softens and expands. A sensuous fragrance flows from your heart, across your chest, and then fills your nostrils with your essence of love. Your loving aroma also carries music of love, sweet tones that whisper love into every cell of your body. Gentle vibrations bring forth your heart's intelligence, ready to heal anything that holds you away from love. You sense an incredible feeling of empowerment and joy. Every new cell generated from this moment will be born in love, balanced and harmonised.

Say to yourself, "I am love, and I am loved." Now, expand your love outward. Place a piece of your love into every sentient being, and feel the entire universe loving you back as you all come together as one. Through our hearts, there is no separation. You will see yourselves in the eyes of all that you meet. Bask in the space of heartfulness for at least a minute.

When ready, breathe soft pink in and out. Each breath draws your heart closer to your physical body. Live with an open heart, connected to the collective intelligence of heartfulness. Your heart is strong and safe. Allow the pink light of love to stay with you for as long as you like. Take two deep breaths in and out. Wiggle your toes and fingers, stretch your body, open your eyes, and smile from your heart.

Journal Work

After you have finished the visualisation, write or draw about any messages you received or sensations you had in or about your heart. How does it feel to have an open heart? How does it feel to have a shield around your heart? Write or draw four ways you show love to others.

Reflections and Actions

Anytime you are overthinking or want to drop into your heart, touch your energetic heart in the middle of your chest with the fingertips of either hand. This touch will direct attention to your heart and away from your mind. Take four deep breaths, close your eyes, and visualise a desire. Then, see and feel yourself living that desire. Stay here for a few minutes, then open your eyes.

Take a healing shower and imagine soft, pink, liquid light flowing from the shower head. Feel it wash away any worries, upsets, or negative energy. Then, feel it sprinkle you with extraordinary healing properties that allow your heart to shine and sparkle as your whole being is cleared and cleansed.

Anytime, even for just a few moments, enter a conversation with your heart. Ask it how it is and if it has any information to share.

8. MEDITATION

Quieten your thoughts and raise your vibes.

Meditation is a gentle shift of attention towards your inner self while breathing consciously. With practice, it becomes easier to quieten thoughts and move into a neutral space where anything is possible.

Message

It is time to begin or resume a meditation practice, to quieten excessive noise and familiarise yourself with the pure you. When inundated with information, allowing it to settle elevates your vibration. This process brings forth information resonating with higher vibes, such as your authentic desires, into your awareness. Whatever doesn't vibe or resonate will fall away from your awareness through lack of attention. Meditation is like closing apps and programs on a device or computer. It frees up space for new desires to enter your awareness.

All meditation teachings and philosophies offer great insights and techniques. There is no right or wrong way to meditate. Consider meditation a gentle shift of attention from the physical world into your inner world of dreams and possibilities while breathing fully and naturally. Over time, you will gain wisdom that encourages you to adjust and master thoughts, emotions, and vibrations. Your inner peace determines your outer experiences.

When meditating, there is no need to push thoughts away. Let them come and go. A cluster of thoughts turns into stories that will compete for your attention. Allow them to do their thing. To calm your thoughts, tell them you will tend to them after your meditation. If you wander into an idea or story, focus on your breath and silently repeat your manifestation name or a word that evokes calm to return to your heart centre.

You can meditate immediately by directing your attention to the card's *taijitu* (*yinyang* symbol), which will transport you to your heart centre. Breathe naturally and soften your gaze. Your perception relaxes, and excessive noise in your mind is reduced. Now, you can bring to your mind something that brings you joy, such as having a massage, playing with your pets, spending time with children, or creating art. Let go and let be.

To cultivate a meditation practice, try out the exercises in the masterclass.

Conscious Creator Masterclass: Building a Meditation Practice

The previous masterclass taught you to give and receive with an open heart by being mindful. You must have an open heart and be present to receive your desires. This masterclass introduces meditation to focus on your heart centre while balancing your thoughts, enabling you to match the vibration of your authentic self and desires.

A Foundation Meditation

I suggest you build up your meditation practice from one, to five, to twenty-four minutes a day — one minute for every hour in a day.

You will need:
- A quiet spot and time, where you won't be disturbed
- A comfortable chair, meditation stool, or cushion (use whatever is most comfortable)
- A candle to light up your inner world
- Your manifestation name or a word that invokes a sense of calm, such as 'calm', 'serene', 'bliss', and 'light'

Optional:
- Gentle music
- Burning incense or aromatherapy oils
- A timer if you have limited time

Meditation apps and timers are great aids for beginners, however, I encourage you to explore your inner world without boundaries or outside influence. Trust your journey. As you practise, you will get to know your inner world through direct experience. Using incense, music, and other ceremonial tools can set a mood that your mind will recognise as a relaxing, safe time and be less likely to disturb the meditation.

The below meditation is a place to begin. You can record yourself on your phone and listen to it as a guided meditation.

Be sure to pause where you know you'll need time to follow the instructions. After a while, meditation will become second nature. When that happens, I urge you to explore other methods to expand your toolbox.

> Sit comfortably in your quiet spot. Maintain a straight and relaxed back. You can sit cross-legged on the floor, on a meditation stool, or cushion.
>
> Close your eyes and bring to mind your manifestation name or word. Repeat it to yourself silently and slowly nine times. Through your nose, take five deep, long breaths in and out. You can use your mouth if your nose is blocked. Chant your manifestation name or word throughout the five breaths. Feel the breath go in and out. The breath of life nourishes your nervous system. With slow breathing, each cell can take what it needs from the air. Allow any thoughts to expand and contract, just like your breath. When you find your mind wandering, use your manifestation name or word and breathe it in five times. Repeat this anytime you feel your mind wandering.
>
> Feel the rise and fall of your chest and stomach. After the five deep, long breaths, breathe naturally and allow a sense of quiet to flow through you. Stay here for as long as you like — at least a minute, building to 24 minutes.
>
> When you are ready to finish, breathe your manifestation name or word into your whole body and mind. Fill yourself up with the breath of life. You are bringing your inner world experiences into your physical world. Be present in your body. Open your eyes and welcome yourself back.

Practise every day. Every meditation, no matter how long or whether it be quiet or noisy, will build your self-worth and a resilient inner world.

Journal Work
Each time you meditate, write a sentence or do a small drawing about one thing you learnt about yourself or what you want to manifest.

Reflections and Actions: Three Ways to Assess Your Meditation Practice Progress

Increased awareness about your mind and reactions
- Do you feel more relaxed and calmer throughout your waking hours?
- Have you discovered which areas of your body hold the most tension so you can deliberately relax them before too much stress builds up?
- Are you becoming more aware of your thoughts and are you able to have more control over them, rather than being controlled by them?
- Have you learnt what things really distract you and therefore can look out for them and avoid getting too scattered?

Improved relationships
- Is your relationship with yourself improving? Are you less critical and kinder to yourself?
- Are your relationships with others improving?
- Are you less likely to be triggered by the actions or words of another?

- Have you softened your resistance to the most challenging people?
- Are you becoming an active listener?
- Have you developed the insight to know when to make changes — i.e., when to set boundaries, or speak your truth and not your judgements, etc.?

Expansion of your consciousness

Inside all of us is a sea of consciousness that we dive into when meditating. Let's define consciousness as the animating force inside us which helps us feel alive and gives us awareness. The size of your consciousness will dictate your view of the world and interactions with it. For instance, if you have an egg-sized consciousness, you will have an egg-sized comprehension when you watch a movie or read a book. Expanding your consciousness will give you more comprehensive access to more profound ideas and understanding.

I began meditation to destress my life but found a new way to live my life. I felt so liberated … like I had come home. I decided I wanted always to feel that way. That decision is still unfolding in my meditation practice.

9. EMOTIONS

Your inner guidance system.

Your emotions are indicators of your vibrational alignment with your desires. They prompt you to make deliberate and gradual adjustments towards feelings that better align with your desires.

Message

You are awash with emotions that are managing your feelings and experience of life. This is their purpose — to act as a feedback system, showing your position in relation to your desires. If you experience something you desire, you feel happy, but if you live through something you don't want, you feel pretty bad. Instead of allowing your emotions to take you on a reactive emotional rollercoaster, let them provide specific feedback about the state of your being so you can respond with a deliberate and gradual adjustment of how you feel.

Emotions result from chemical processes produced by your thoughts. Feelings are states of consciousness experienced as a result of an emotion. Whatever you feel right now is where you are — it is neither right nor wrong. There is no need to push it away or pull it towards you. Take a deep breath and gently focus on the card's image. Imagine you are the figure in the picture, sitting with the awareness of your feelings that flow from your 'e-motions' (energy in motion — the vibrations and frequency that flow from you).

Be gentle with yourself and take small steps. When you care about your feelings, you will automatically find a better way to master your emotions. As you master your emotions and feelings, you can create an inner atmosphere and picture filled with your desires. If you think and believe it, you will feel and attract it.

Explore the exercises in the masterclass to embody the message and feel your way into better feelings.

Conscious Creator Masterclass: Initiating Your Inner Technology

The previous masterclass introduced meditation to focus on your heart centre while balancing your thoughts, which enables you to match the vibration of your authentic self and desires. This masterclass introduces your emotions' unique wisdom and teaches you to shift them into something more aligned with your desires.

Visualisation

Find a place to sit down. Place your hands on your lap face up, with the *Emotions* card between your feet. In your mind, repeat your manifestation name or the words 'I feel' nine times. Close your eyes softly and tenderly. Focus on the middle of your chest and imagine floating on a wave of sacred geometry that leads to your heart. Breathe in and out of your heart.

Deep within your heart, a point of light grows. It grows larger and larger until you can gently float into this exquisite space. Your temple of inner technology materialises.

It is so bright, beautiful, and inviting. You float up the stairs and enter your temple, where you are greeted by sweet music and clouds of beautiful colours containing symbols and geometric shapes. You are drawn to a nearby wall. The words 'Your Inner Guidance' appear across the top of the wall, written in giant, bold letters. Underneath is a huge sliding scale, taking up the entire length of the wall. There is a brass indicator that you can move backwards and forwards along the scale. At one end of the scale is 'joy', and at the other end is 'despair'. In between are many other positive and negative emotions spread evenly along the scale. Whichever emotion you select on the brass indicator, you will experience.

Move the indicator to 'joy'. Allow that feeling to move through you. Bask in its energy and get to know its vibration and frequency so you can tune in to it whenever you want. Now, move the indicator to 'despair'. Allow that contrasting feeling to move through you. Take a breath and stay here momentarily to recognise its vibration so you can deliberately shift to something that feels better. Move the indicator back to something lighter.

Now, spend as much time as you want to explore the feeling and vibrations of your emotions by experimenting with the slide and different emotions. There is an array of human emotions to meet. Learning how they feel in your body empowers you and your manifestation skills.

When ready, place your indicator on the emotion that empowered you and thank your temple for its offerings. This is your temple; it has and will always exist within you, and you can visit whenever you like. Each time you visit, you will expand upon previous experiences and empower your wisdom and inner technology.

A wave of loving vibrations takes you back to your heart. Breathe deeply and feel your consciousness fill your body through your heart. Wiggle your toes and fingers. Stretch your body and open your eyes.

Journal Work

After you have completed the visualisation, write or draw a list of any emotions you experienced as you went through the exercise. Go through the list one by one and write or draw about the following: Where in your body do you experience the emotion? What does it feel like? Is there a colour, sound, or story attached to the emotion? You are familiarising yourself with your inner world of vibrations and frequency.

Reflections and Actions

Your body is a vibrator! It receives and transmits vibrational information. Emotions are the movement of energy, transmitting unique frequencies of vibration. Here are three steps to use your inner guidance system.

1. How do you feel right now?

List the top three emotions you feel right now. Turn towards your feelings with curiosity and without judgement. All emotions have worth and are valid. Honour the emotions that created a feeling, good or bad, and thank them for alerting you to how you feel.

2. Identify and label the emotion
To stay mindful and gain the most information from the emotion, say, "This is joy," or "This is anger." You already know how this emotion feels from step one. Using "this is" diminishes the intensity of the story triggered by the emotion. You are learning more about your inner world and refining your desires.

3. Reach for the next highest feeling emotion
You have felt the emotion and identified it. The next step is to shift it to a higher vibration. Take one step at a time. Feel it, name it, and then move to the next highest feeling emotion. For example, anger feels better than despair, blame feels better than anger, irritation feels better than blame, pessimism feels better than irritation, optimism feels better than pessimism, hope feels better than optimism, joy feels better than hope, and bliss feels better than joy.

Celebrate each step you take. You deliberately shift your vibration from resistance to allowance to receive your desires. You are also training yourself to feel your best on the way to all you desire. This is a form of self-love and care.

If you want to dive deeper into understanding different levels and vibrations of emotions, research Dr. David R. Hawkins' 'Map of Consciousness' or Abraham–Hicks' 'Emotional Guidance Scale'.

10. SOUL PERSPECTIVE

The future is seen within.

Elevate your perception to view your desires through the eyes of your soul and your next steps will become clear. You'll recognise the right vibration by a sense of 'this feels right' even if your mind believes differently.

Message

You will soon find it easier to raise your vibration and tune in to the loving wisdom of your soul. When you relax, meditate, or deliberately shift your emotional state to a higher frequency, you lift yourself beyond the layers of outdated beliefs around your soul. Look at the card's image and imagine this is you and your soul aligned. This is your authentic nature, and infinite possibilities are possible from this space.

No parts of your being will feel separated when you reunite with your whole, authentic higher self. It will feel like you are having a natural conversation with yourself because you and your soul vibrate simultaneously. When you align and tune in, a stream of higher visions and inspired action will convey to you ways to manifest your desires, solutions, or a pathway to resources to heal any issues in your life.

If something doesn't feel right, or you blame situations or others for feeling tetchy, you and your soul are looking at the same thing but interpreting it differently. Your emotional reactions combine your thoughts and your soul's thoughts. When they don't align, you are resisting what is happening now. Inadvertently, you overlay a story, interpretation, or conclusion that splits and distances yourself from the present moment. You might not see both sides, but your soul does. It allows all things to be simply as they are.

When you have the same perspective as your soul, things feel *right*, satisfactory, and easy. You go with the flow. Your soul will never join you in judgement, blame, or hurt because that is not the perspective of love. How you feel reveals how aligned you are with your soul; check in with your emotions and reach for a better feeling emotion. If you are experiencing something that doesn't feel quite right, take a breath and return to your centre. You will feel better and inspired to navigate your inner radar, ready to receive transmissions from your soul.

Explore the exercises in the masterclass to embody the message and feel your way into your soul's viewpoint.

Conscious Creator Masterclass: Raising Your Perspective

The previous masterclass presented your inner guidance system and the unique wisdom that your emotions and feelings offer. This masterclass introduces 'love' as your soul's natural perspective and how to use your emotions to lift your perspective and align with soul love.

This visualisation uses a technique called 'the violet flame'. It is a cool fire of transformation. Anything that passes through the violet flames moves into a higher vibration of love. You can invoke it anytime you want to transform or transmute lower energies into higher ones. It lives within you.

Visualisation

Find a comfortable place to sit down. Place the *Soul Perspective* card at your feet. In your mind, repeat your manifestation name or the words 'my soul' nine times. Gently close your eyes. Sense your body and concentrate on your breathing. Feel your consciousness flow in the stream of the present moment. Thoughts come and go. Awareness likes to move from one thing to another because it seeks something. Just notice if your mind wanders and observe where it may be going. Notice that you are the watcher and can choose where to direct your attention. Breathe deeply and relax.

Imagine breathing shades of violet, blue, and gold and allowing these colours to move through you like a gentle warmth touching every part of you with mystic wisdom. Feel into the eternal moment happening now ... and now ... and now ... Enter your sacred centre — your soul perspective; it may be in your heart, your solar plexus, your mind, your mind's eye or even your big toe. Wherever it is, take yourself there. Breathe gold into this place. Allow all to be as it is and sink deeper into your beauty. Dive deeper and allow your riches—infinite unconditional love—to be illuminated and revealed. Let go, let it be.

From your sacred centre, witness the viewpoint of your soul. A violet flame reveals itself. Allow any unwanted thoughts, pain, hurt, ideas, old stories, experiences, or situations to pass through the flame, one at a time. Watch or feel it flicker as each thing dissolves, then transforms into love, creating tiny sparks of gold and white light that leap from the flame. Keep passing items through the violet flame for as long as you like.

You have transcended the old and become the love that ripples out from you to inspire others to release what no longer serves them, if they so desire. You feel lighter, renewed, and full of inspired action. Gently float from your sacred centre.

Take this with you as you connect with your breath. Breathe in shades of violet, blue, and gold until you feel fully present. Wiggle your toes and fingers, stretch your body, and open your eyes.

Journal Work

After the visualisation, choose one or two of your unwanted thoughts, pain, hurt, ideas, old stories, experiences, or situations. Then write or draw how you feel now after passing them through the violet flame. This journal work will support you moving towards and recognising your soul perspective.

Reflections and Actions

As each moment passes, your life experiences integrate, and your wisdom expands. You are perfect just as you are, right here and right now. In every moment, you embody the culmination of all your experiences. While your thoughts may evolve from those of your childhood, a year ago, or even yesterday, you will always recognise the core of who you are.

Your soul is pure, non-resistant energy. For one day, imagine you see the world through the eyes of your soul. If you feel yourself reacting, stop. Take a breath and ask your soul what it sees and if it has any solutions to share. Have fun with this, you may be surprised.

Maybe you are noticing many more glimpses of your soul's perspective. If it resonates, work with it. If not, just put it in your back pocket, and one day it will make sense.

II. REMEMBRANCE

Recognise and recollect your deepest desires.

The activation of forgotten memories of your soul's truth and your purpose. Unite all aspects of yourself that open your heart, mind, and body to recall that you can create something fresh and distinct.

Message

Glimpses of your soul's desires are peeking through your heart and showing up, or soon will be, as 11:11 or a combination of 1s — for example, 1:11, 11:10, or 11. You may see it on a clock, phone number, receipt, or in a dream. Stop what you are doing when you see it and ask, "What is in my heart?" Then, be open to receiving fresh and innovative ideas that will gently blend more of your authentic self with your desires and goals.

When you landed on Earth, your fullness was veiled so that you could remember it through the perspective of your earthly life and embrace all parts. Give a big welcome to all your different aspects, let them in and hug them. You are gaining information and tools that will prepare you to remember the totality of your truth.

Every 11:11 encounter will bring new information and ideas swirling within you. No one can tell you what 11:11 means to you. It has many meanings because we ask many different questions, based on our lives and experiences. But at the heart of 11:11 is a loving, intelligent energy that will always encourage you into complete alignment with yourself, so that you can feel the truth of yourself and create from your aligned potential. If you are reading this, 11:11 wants you to know that you have the courage to live from your heart, discover a new world, and inspire others to remember their soul truth.

Explore the exercises in the masterclass to embody the message and feel your way into remembrance through your heart temple.

Conscious Creator Masterclass: Exploring 11:11 In Your Heart Temple

The previous masterclass explained how to lift your vibration to see your soul's perspective. This masterclass introduces using 11:11 to feel into your soul's heart and remember your deeper truths. Codes of light exist in your inner temple and all temples worldwide, waiting to be remembered.

Visualisation

Find a comfortable place to sit down. Place the *Remembrance* card between your feet on the floor. In your mind, repeat your manifestation name or the word 'remember' nine times. Tune in to your breathing and slow it down. Imagine your breath is shimmering blue and violet light. Breathe deeply, filling yourself with light and breathe it out to fill the entire space around you. Brilliant blue-violet light softens every part of your mind. Words, thoughts, and distractions float away on waves of light, and your mind becomes quiet. You feel deeply loved and peaceful.

As you relax into your light, the symbol 11:11 floats before you. The numerals shift and dance like loving angels, drawing you towards the dots in the middle. Focus on these dots. It becomes a point of golden light that grows. Expanding outward, it pushes the 1s apart to reveal a magnificent temple with the words 'know thy heart' over the doorway.

You are standing at the edge of your perception, but you feel a sense of familiarity and realise it is your soul urging you forwards. Light pours from the entrance, embraces and gently floats you into the temple. Within the temple, you are showered with golden light. This is the light of your soul, and in this magical space, you and your soul become one.

A full remembrance of yourself activates, your consciousness expands, and a paradigm shift will soon occur. From now on you will always recognise who you are, becoming more of yourself. Each time you enter this journey, you become more; you expand into infinite space to create, manifest, and play in a world you manifest from your heart. Let this become a part of your vibrational reality. Know that all you desire and more will manifest into your physical reality; now that you know this, you can relax and enjoy life. Bask in the space of your soul remembrance for at least a minute.

Call your consciousness back to your physical self. Feel your awareness leaving your heart temple, moving through the dots between 11:11, then floating on your blue-violet light and merging with your heart. Allow your consciousness to flow from your heart and expand into every cell within your body. What you experienced is now a part of every cell and, from now on, all new cells will be born from love.

Take two deep breaths in and out. Wiggle your toes and fingers, stretch your body, open your eyes, and smile.

Journal Work

After the visualisation, write or draw what your heart temple looked and felt like, as well as any other messages you received from your heart and 11:11.

You may like to add a section in your journal called 11:11. When you experience this pattern, note the date. Under this, draw or write about your experience and any messages you received. Recording your encounters will reveal patterns of information or ideas.

Reflections and Actions

Some call 11:11 an awakening code. You must have awoken on some level to receive it. It is a sign that you are much more than you believe you are. Remember, there is no right or wrong meaning of 11:11. It means something different for everyone. 11:11 brings a loving, intelligent energy encouraging you towards your soul truth.

The symbolic energy of 1 is filled with new beginnings, innovation, and leadership. The next time you encounter 11:11, take five minutes to record four ways you can improve your life. Instead of making a wish, use your encounter with 11:11 to affirm and declare to the universe, "I know I deserve [your want], and I am open to receiving the steps to make it happen. Thank you." You have just become an active part of creating your desire.

12. ALIGNMENT

Your mind, heart, and gut are in agreement.

The easiest way to know if you are in alignment is by the way you feel. When you sense a big "yes", you align with your desire. Being out of alignment is a natural consequence of new experiences, which reveal preferences.

Message

You are gaining the ability to align with, and translate, the language of your soul as it flows from your heart. As you attune to the perspective of your soul—also referred to as your higher self—you gain access to your soul wisdom through the intuitive impulses of the heart. Your energetic heart is a neutral space where your power and the doorway to all desires exist. Your soul is your biggest fan. It understands your higher purpose and sees the vibrational reality of your dreams and desires. It pulses this information through your feelings and emotions to lovingly guide you onto the path of most allowance towards your desires.

Your mind, heart, and gut must agree to receive the information about the path of least resistance. You will know this when what you think and feel have a similar goal. For example, you think, "It's time to go for a walk." You feel, "It would be lovely to be outside and move my body." The momentum of inspired action quickly moves you to do this, and you say, "A walk is the best thing for me to do right now." And off you go. Being aligned is pleasurable, truthful, satisfactory, and accessible — a strong feeling that all is well.

Other ways to create an aligned state are meditating, repeating your manifestation name, enjoying something you love, or napping. You can also focus on the heart in the middle of the image and ask your mind, heart, and gut to meet there.

When life experiences pull you out of alignment, feeling a little shaky or wobbly is normal. This is a natural process to help you gain a new perspective and improve clarity about your desires. When you are feeling out of alignment, ask questions that guide you towards creating a new balance. Being out of alignment can feel awful. It is easy to blame a person or situation when we feel bad, but instead of asking why something is happening, ask what you can create from the situation to improve your life and the lives of others. And remember, your soul is continually in alignment; it is a consistent, loving home you can return to.

Explore the exercises in the masterclass to embody the message and experience ways to align with your heart and desires.

Conscious Creator Masterclass: Alignment Enlightens Soul Desires

The previous masterclass presented 11:11 to feel into your heart and remember your deepest truths. This masterclass introduces the concept of alignment. The way to bring your mind, body, and spirit into alignment to access the path of most allowance through your emotions and feelings.

Visualisation

Place the *Alignment* card between your feet on the floor. Place your hands on your energetic heart in the middle of your chest. In your mind, repeat your manifestation name or the word 'align' nine times. Gently close your eyes. Sense your body, mind, and spirit, and concentrate on your breathing. Direct love to your physical heart and give thanks for its rhythm of life. Consciously relax every part of you.

Settle your awareness in the middle of your chest. Draw your manifestation name or word across your chest. From deep within your heart, a tiny point of light grows. It flows outward through the middle of your name or word. Direct it to the outside of your body and ask it to expand to a bubble of light that surrounds your entire body. You are floating in your heart space within this transparent bubble. The air is clear, cleansing, light, and healing. It is easy to take long, deep, nourishing breaths. You feel safe, relaxed, and calm.

You feel your mind, body, and spirit shifting and moving. Ask them to align at the point of your manifestation name or word. You feel them actively choosing to meet where you have asked them to. Suddenly, you feel a subtle click and know they are all lined up with your soul's desires. Alignment has intensified the surrounding frequencies, turning them into coloured waves of light that bathe you. Everything you desire is here; you connect to this feeling and knowing by simply being aware of it. Play in this space for at least two minutes to stabilise the sense of alignment.

Focus on the outside of your bubble and draw it inward until it becomes the tiny point of light again. Let it flow into your heart. It contains all the information you have just experienced which will live within your heart. Notice that your manifestation name or word has transformed into the word 'LOVE'. When you want to feel aligned, direct your attention to your heart and breathe. Breathe deeply and bring your awareness back to your physical body, wiggle your toes and fingers, and open your eyes.

Journal Work
After you have completed the visualisation, write or draw what the feeling of alignment reminds you of. This will help ground the sensation into your nervous system so you can easily recall what the sense tells you.

Reflections and Actions
Try alternate nostril breathing. It's a great way to align and reset.

1. Sit comfortably in a quiet space and relax with your non-dominant hand in your lap.
2. Raise your other hand to your face, and place your index, middle, and ring fingers between your eyebrows. You will leave them here for the remainder of the exercise. You will be only moving your thumb and pinky finger.

3. Close your eyes and take a deep breath in and out of your nose.
4. Close the nostril with your thumb on one nostril and inhale slowly and steadily.
5. Removing the thumb, close the other nostril with your pinky finger and exhale. When finished, inhale through this same nostril.
6. Removing the pinky finger, close the nostril with the thumb and exhale slowly and steadily.
7. Repeat the cycle at least two more times and up to ten times.

Do some research on other types of breathwork or try a class or workshop. My favourite is holotropic breathwork.

Try some cross-crawl exercises, which are great for bringing balance to your body. Cross-crawl exercises can be as simple as marching on the spot. They involve movements that require the left and right sides of the body to work together while completing opposing actions. Do some research. There are many easy ways to do these exercises.

13. THE PRINCIPLE OF ATTRACTION

What goes out returns to you.

The principle of attraction is the attractive magnetic power of the universe that draws similar energies and vibrations together. It manifests through the creation process in many ways, such as emotions, ideas, actions, or events.

Message

Here is a clear message for you, delivered by the principle of attraction: "You are the creator of the way you feel, and the way you feel creates your environment, inside and out." The principle of attraction holds no judgment; it simply brings you more of what you offer.

Everything in the universe, including thoughts, emotions, and physical objects, has its own distinct vibration or energy signature. The universal principle of attraction uses these signatures to determine alignment and bring things together. You have a unique energy frequency—your core vibration, also known as your Manifestation Name—that shapes what you attract. This core vibration acts as an energetic fingerprint, formed by the invisible energy signatures and resonances of your accumulated beliefs and thoughts, continuously influencing your interactions and experiences.

To understand the universe's perspective, imagine looking into a mirror that reflects your physical appearance and vibrational self, displaying your desires, thoughts, and beliefs as energy patterns. This vibrational language is how the universe communicates with you.

The principle of attraction is always at work, like gravity—we see the results even if we can't see the process. Your life reveals how you feel about outcomes so you can refine your energy and what you attract. Imagine your future self or desire is complete and pulling you towards it. Every decision you make now supports and creates your future self or desire. Care about how you feel by choosing thoughts that help you feel better, focusing on the qualities of your desires, and finding where they are present in your life now.

Explore the exercises in the masterclass to embody the message of attraction.

Conscious Creator Masterclass: Observing Magnetic Attraction

The previous masterclass presented the concept of alignment — bringing your mind, body, and spirit into alignment to access the path of most allowance through your emotions and feelings. This masterclass activates a remembrance in your heart about the principle of attraction.

Visualisation

Find a comfortable place to sit or lie down. Place *The Principle of Attraction* card at your feet. In your mind, repeat your manifestation name or the word 'attraction' nine times. Gently close your eyes. Sense your body and concentrate on your breathing. Follow your breath inward. Hold for five seconds. Breathe out and release all tension. Relax and breathe naturally.

Imagine yourself floating on an ocean of white light. You feel so calm and relaxed. Visualise the colours in the image as waves of blue, pink, and green being magnetically drawn to you. This is what your desires look like as frequencies in the non-physical realm. As the waves of colour move closer to your heart, they form shapes. Moving closer to the physical, they shift and morph into matter that resembles your desires.

As you float upon an ocean of white, all around you are different versions of yourself living all your dreams. You float among them, observing and feeling your desires. They seem so real, and this realness makes them seem possible. Take in all the sights, sounds, smells, and emotions of your future self, living your best life. Explore for at least a minute.

The scene becomes smaller and smaller until you can pick it up and place it in your heart. The future self that you just experienced has now become a magnet that pulls you towards it. Every decision you make from now until then will support your dreams and desires. The ocean of white light transforms into matter that you recognise as your body. Feel yourself merging with your magnificent physical body.

Take two deep breaths in and out. Wiggle your toes and fingers, stretch your body, and open your eyes. Welcome to a new world.

Journal Work

After the visualisation, jot down or sketch the elements you encountered or witnessed converging to manifest your desires. Then, write or draw about what areas of your life you are most confident in and consider how you can apply that certainty to areas that may be shaky.

This will help you become a magnet for vibrations and frequencies that are more aligned with your desires.

Reflections and Actions

There are three parts to the Law of Attraction: ask, align, and allow.

Ask: Once you have asked for your desire, the universe weaves its magic to bring it to you. There is no need to keep asking or searching for evidence of your desire; this will hold your vibration in the asking phase. You can check in with your manifestation name. Have a dialogue with it: ask how this desire will improve your life and if there is a better way to create the feeling you seek from your desire.

Align: Your work is to align with the vibes of most allowance. You can shift your vibration by shifting your thoughts and feelings (check out the card *Alignment*). You will know where you are vibrating by the way you feel. If there are things you don't like, start changing them. If you can't change them, walk away. If you can't walk away, change your perception. If you find yourself on the lower end of emotions, gently reach for a better-feeling thought. Negative doesn't mean bad — it is just a place to align with your desire. Pat yourself on the back for being aware and waiting to master your inner creator. Vision boards, visualisations, or guided meditations will help maintain a stable alignment.

Allow: If you were inspired to ask, you are worthy of getting what you want. Open your arms to your desire by aligning your awareness to what feels good, inside and out, as you go about your daily life. In this heightened, aligned-vibe awareness, you will notice synchronicities, coincidences, and inspired actions that will move you towards the path of most allowance. You are ready to experience your desire and its variants. To manifest it is to allow it in.

14. CREATE YOUR WORLD

Think your dreams into reality.

You activate your inner creator when you use your imagination to design a desired life. Believing it is possible opens a door for it to manifest in surprising, fulfilling, and satisfying ways. If you dream it and believe it, you will create it.

Message

You have been waiting for something to change so you can feel better. This inadvertently puts your happiness into the hands of another person or system, and you hope they will create something you want to live in. Your life will always be what you believe your life will be, so create one that brings you joy. The power of your mind is compelling. Be open to the possibility that your desires are possible and see what happens!

"Your thoughts create your reality" is an accurate statement, but maybe not in the way you believe. The idea of, "I want this thing, so I put in my order," has derived from commercialism, as you are asking to exchange your thoughts for a desire. Instead, think of your mind as a transmitter and receiver. It translates your thoughts into vibration and frequency waves. What you emit through the waves is a combination of your thoughts, how you feel, and who you are when you think that thought.

For instance, imagine feeling anxious and running into an acquaintance who asks how you are. Your immediate response is, "I'm fine, thanks," yet you're still tense beneath the surface. This nervous vibration is palpable to others, leading them to question, "Are you sure?" Sensing your discomfort, they offer you a chance to open up. At this point, you have the choice to shape your reality. You might respond honestly: "Actually, I'm feeling anxious today. Thank you for asking; it helps." While it may require courage, such authenticity dissipates anxiety, freeing you to explore new thoughts or actions. By taking responsibility without assigning blame, you empower yourself and your journey.

Picture the universe emerging from the Source's mind. All visible forms, including yourself, are diverse thoughts emanating from this Source. Although it may seem abstract, realising the universe's eternal nature and your connection to Source empowers you to shape reality and craft your own world.

Explore the exercises in the masterclass to embody the message and experience new ways of thinking.

Conscious Creator Masterclass: Being Present to Know Your Mind

The previous masterclass presented the principle of attraction. This masterclass introduces your ability to change anything by what you think.

Visualisation

Accessing your mind when you are present in your body is more effortless. Before you begin the visualisation try this: ask your manifestation name or the word 'witness' to be an observer of your mind and ask it what it sees. Take your focus to the top of your head, scan your body slowly, and release any tension, tightness, or stress. Breathe deeply and direct your awareness to your mind. This is a form of mindfulness. (Check out *Heartfulness* for more info on mindfulness.)

Find a comfortable place to sit or lie down. Place the *Create Your World* card at your feet. In your mind, repeat your manifestation name or the word 'witness' nine times. Gently close your eyes. Sense your body and concentrate on your breathing. Follow your breath inward. Hold for five seconds. Breathe out and release all tension. Relax and breathe naturally.

Imagine your favourite colour filling the room and moving like a gentle mist around you. Travelling on the waves of your colour is a feeling of relaxation and calm. As your colour moves around you, you begin to breathe it in, and you become so relaxed and calm.

Direct your colour to flow over the front of you. It is relaxing and calming the whole front side of you. Any thoughts or fears about the future gently float away as you engage in the here and now.

Direct your colour to flow down over the back of you. It is relaxing and calming the whole back side of you. Your past gently floats away as you become absorbed in the here and now.

In the here and now, the eternal mind unfolds and projects a picture of your biggest desire. Watch the movie of your desire. How do you feel? Is it everything you want? Imagine that you can change anything about your desire. In your mind, think something different about the scenario and see how it plays out. Albert Einstein called these 'thought experiments'. Watch, feel, and become your genius mind playing with the possibilities of your desires for the fun of it. Stay here for at least two minutes.

When you feel ready, breathe your projected desires into your heart. Breathe your colour into your body. It will consistently create relaxation and calm and return you to the present moment. You can change your thoughts and desires to align with your up-to-date authentic self in the here and now. Take two deep breaths in and out. Wiggle your toes and fingers, stretch your body, open your eyes, and smile.

Journal Work
After the visualisation, write or draw about the desire you projected and if you changed anything about it. To emphasise awareness of thought and your mind, write or draw about your thoughts. Then, write or draw how you would finish this sentence: "I live in a thinking universe, and I feel ..."

Reflections and Actions
Consider the impulses and thoughts that led you to this deck. What is the thought influencing your mood right now? Become mindful so you are not creating your life mindlessly.

Trust a decision and let it be. Constantly turning it over in your mind will introduce doubt. Soon enough, you will see the results and can decide on your next steps. As new pathways form, old ones naturally weaken and fall away. Eventually, through repetition, your new pathways will run on autopilot. You may benefit from researching Socratic thinking, rational thinking, or Byron Katie's work.

Research neuroplasticity to understand how your brain can change and rewire itself in response to new experiences and the learning that comes from them.

Research the Reticular Activating System, part of the brain stem that functions to filter out uninteresting input so that irrelevant details do not overwhelm you. It keeps your attention on anything deemed essential or that you are focused on. Your mind sees reflected information and evidence that validates your beliefs. For example, if you think about yellow cars, you will see them wherever you go.

15. ATTRACTION POINT

An assembly of dominant beliefs and emotions.

The accumulation of your beliefs, knowledge, and experiences shapes your perception of reality and personality, attracting similar vibrations and frequencies.

Message

You are becoming more confident in expressing your passions, creating a brighter, more genuine attraction point that makes it easier for your desires and their components to locate you. These components could be anything that turns up in your life, such as a sign, symbol, overheard conversation, a book falling from a shelf, people who want to help, or different experiences. Now that you know this, you will become more aware of synchronicities and the magical chain of events that bring the pieces together to inspire new paths, ideas, and actions that will lead to your desires more quickly.

Your attraction point is the combination of your beliefs, knowledge, and experiences that shape your perception of reality and your personality. It's the accumulation of your most predominant thoughts that resonate out from you, some of which you are aware of, and some you are not. The latter are thoughts you have repeated so often that they have become embodied beliefs.

Your attraction point helps you frame the world around you based on your experiences and conclusions, so you can feel a sense of safety — but it's more flexible than you might think. You can change any part of your beliefs, knowledge, and stories, and shift your attraction point.

If you are still determining your attraction point, observe your life, the people around you, and your work. Is life moving in the direction you desire? A teacher once told me I had dog energy — loyal to every group I interacted with but not faithful to my soul. My attraction point was being influenced by the belief that no one would accept or love me if I were to be my true self. I pretended to be something to please others until I awoke to my behaviour.

The downwards-pointing triangle in the card's image represents your soul collecting and clarifying your dreams, where your mind translates them as desires. The upwards-pointing triangle signifies the components and elements—non-physical and physical—that resonate with your desires. When these two come together, vibrational waves radiate as your delicious passions. This is the attraction point of your desire.

Explore the exercises in the masterclass to embody the message and become an attraction point for your desires.

Conscious Creator Masterclass: Attractive Components at Play

The previous masterclass presented your ability to change anything by how you think. This masterclass introduces the concept that through your attraction point, you draw the components needed to bring your desire into being, while inspiring others to do the same.

Visualisation

Find a comfortable place to sit or lie down. Place the *Attraction Point* card at your feet. In your mind, repeat your manifestation name or the word 'bring' nine times. Gently close your eyes. Sense your body and concentrate on your breathing. Follow your breath inward. Hold for five seconds. Breathe out and release all tension. Relax and breathe naturally. Take your focus to the place between your eyebrows, your third eye. Breathe into your third eye to open and activate it. Focus all your awareness here and imagine you gently slip behind your physical eyes to see into the mind of the universe.

You are surrounded by nebulous, colourful clouds in pink, blue, purple, and orange hues. Two golden triangles come into your vision — one pointing upwards, the other pointing down. They are floating towards each other slowly and deliberately. You watch the two triangles come together with a click, like a spaceship docking in space, to create a star. Gently float into your attraction point at the centre of the star. You remain calm, in a state of harmony, understanding that being present here, magnetically attracts all that is necessary to manifest your desire.

A shimmering light being materialises in front of you to help you understand the process of co-creating. You float together, observing the facilitation of a desire. You witness a person offering a specific frequency that you see as colour waves and symbols. Then, you see someone on the other side of the planet offering a similar frequency. You watch in amazement as a timeline is created that connects them through space. Colourful waves organise geometric elements along the timeline through specific events so these two people can meet and facilitate each other's desires.

From this higher vantage point, your light being guides your attention to your physical self, living out your life. Incredibly, you witness your attraction point as waves of colour and shapes which form events and synchronicities that lead to your desires. Pledge to embrace and action these opportunities, as they are here to help you manifest your desires. Take at least a minute to observe with gentle attention.

Your light being embraces you and fades from view; this is not goodbye, you'll see them again. Your star becomes smaller until you can place it in your heart. You move through the nebulous, colourful clouds into your physical awareness. As the light floats away, you sense the word 'remember' reverberating through you. Allow the light of curiosity and wisdom to stay with you for as long as you like. Take two deep breaths in and out. Wiggle your toes and fingers, stretch your body, and open your eyes.

Journal Work

After the visualisation, write or draw about what you observed. Then, write or draw the emotions or feelings you experienced during the visualisation. These will help you tune in to and recognise the components that your attraction point draws to you.

Reflections and Actions
Do the following exercise to bring clarity and change to your attraction point.
- Choose something you desire.
- For 10 seconds, focus on how it feels to have this desire.
- Then try doing this for 20 seconds. Keep adding 10-second increments until your focus wanes.
- When this happens, note what you thought about. You may find it to be the predominant vibrations of your attraction point.
- Practise thinking about your desire for a week and see if you can go further.
- Work up to five minutes. Holding this for five minutes will begin a momentum that shifts your attraction point to your new focus, and all other focusses will fall away from lack of attention.

How to gain wisdom and improve your relationship with trees
Next time you are in a park, forest, or the bush, you will feel the impulse to ask what tree has a message for you. Close your eyes and scan the area with your inner eye and imagination. Your attraction point will draw you towards a particular tree. Open your eyes and walk to the tree. Sit with it and ask what it wants to share with you. When you have finished, thank the tree for all it does. We breathe the oxygen they give out as they breathe the carbon dioxide we breathe out. What an excellent co-creative relationship.

16. VIBRATION

Everything moves to a unique frequency.

Everything is energy, and everything has a vibrational signature that is part of an interconnected web of electromagnetic vibrational frequencies. The molecules in your body vibrate constantly, creating electromagnetic waves that emit energy. Emotions, attitude, and perception influence vibrational frequencies.

Message

The way you translate your vibrations is being upgraded. At present, you do it by feeling the 'vibe' of a room, place, or person; you know something, but you're not sure how you came to that conclusion. Your upgrade will reveal what you have had all along — an internal emotional guidance system, which is the most sophisticated way to sense and understand the subtle frequencies of vibration. Check out the *Emotions* card to learn more about this.

The universe doesn't 'speak' a language, it emits frequencies of vibrational waves. If you amplify the frequency, the structure of matter will change. In other words, the better you feel, the more you open the door to your higher wisdom; the worse you feel, the more you shut this door. When you pay attention to your emotions, you better understand the vibrations you transmit. You'll sense your alignment with your soul's perspective and intentionally shift your emotions to uplift your mood and alter your vibrations. This allows you to connect with your soul essence, gaining deeper insight into your identity and the reasons behind your life's events.

Basic science tells us atoms are in constant motion — everything you experience in your physical environment is vibrating, including you. Imagine for a moment that your senses are translating the surrounding vibrations into what you see, touch, hear, smell, and taste. This could answer the philosophical thought experiment: "If a tree fell in the forest and no one was there to hear it, would it make a sound?" The falling tree would cause a vibration. However, without a sensory apparatus (such as your ears) to translate the vibration, it would not be heard. Just let that settle into your awareness and feel your vibration rising.

Explore the exercises in the masterclass to embody the message and feel your way into different frequencies of vibration.

Conscious Creator Masterclass: Feeling Emotional Vibrations

The previous masterclass presented the idea that you draw the components needed to bring your desire into being while inspiring others to do the same, because of your point of attraction. This masterclass introduces the world of vibration and how your emotions and feelings offer a way to align with your soul and desires.

Visualisation

Find a comfortable place to sit or lie down. Place the *Vibration* card at your feet. In your mind, repeat your manifestation name or the word 'vibrate' nine times. Gently close your eyes. Sense your body and concentrate on your breathing. Follow your breath inward. Hold for five seconds. Breathe out and release all tension. Relax and breathe naturally.

Imagine your favourite colour rising around you. Breathe it in and flow it through your whole body. How does it feel? Allow a word to arise in your mind that describes the feeling. It could also be your manifestation name. Now sense the feeling expanding, embracing you, drawing you deeper and deeper into your soul wisdom until you are standing in front of a door labelled 'Feel Your Vibes Room'. Open the door and enter.

Scattered on the walls are many buttons labelled with different emotions. You notice they are arranged from fear to joy, including anger, frustration, hope, passion, and many more. When you push a button, your body floods with the feeling of that emotion and its accompanying colour. You can visit this room anytime to sense a feeling or add new emotional buttons. Play with as many buttons as you like for at least a few minutes.

Now that you know how an emotion feels, you can easily tune your frequency towards your preferred feeling. Tune in to an emotion that creates a sense of liberation and connection to your soul. Step out of the room, breathe in your favourite colour again and float on its frequency waves back to your body. Wiggle your toes and fingers. Then, stretch your body and open your eyes.

Journal Work

After the visualisation, write or draw a list of the emotions you played with. Then, write or draw if any of the realised feelings surprised you. For example, I used to think a certain feeling was anxiety. When I questioned it and dove into the feeling, I realised it was passionate excitement. I had mislabelled it. As I investigated further, I uncovered a pattern. Whenever I was passionate about doing something, I was told I couldn't do it or wasn't worthy of it. When I have that feeling now, I say to myself, "This is something important to me, and I won't know the outcome until I do it. Only then can I decide if it is for me. It will lead me to something even better if it isn't."

Reflections and Actions

Your voice vibrates through space and time, so learn to speak in a way that you know will impact others in a generative manner. Integrate what you've learnt so it becomes part of your everyday life, no longer something outside of you or something new — it is part of who you are.

Other ways to raise your vibration are:

- Ask your manifesting name what it wants to share with you.
- Practise meditation, mindfulness, heartfulness, or breathwork. Any of these will quieten your thoughts. When your thoughts are quieter, resistance dissolves, and your energy rises.
- Make and use a vision board. Imagine your goal, shift your vibration to match it and feel all your decisions aligning with your goal's frequency.
- Be kind and smile; your vibration will naturally rise when you do either.

- Stand barefoot on the earth or hug a tree to ground yourself, which gives you the foundation to rise higher.
- Drink water and eat whole foods to fill yourself with a high vibrational lifeforce.
- Stand outside in the sun for five minutes each morning to wake yourself up and allow light to enter your eyes.
- Write your own ...

17. DANCING WITH YOUR RHYTHM

Being in flow with your desires.

Let go of any 'shoulds, woulds, or coulds' and breathe deeply into the rhythm of your soul. Your mind won't step on your toes when you dance with your soul.

Message

Your heart is astounding; its rhythm maintains your body for you to experience life. Likewise, your heart chakra—the multi-dimensional source of your soul wisdom and intelligence—floats in the centre of your chest. It resonates with invisible waves of rhythmic creation. These are visible to your inner world. The creation of a desire and the subsequent emotions form vibrational waves that expand and contract through space and time. When you are in rhythm and sync, you are surfing the waves of dreams and know when to take inspired action. You will feel what needs to be released or embraced to create the path towards the fullness of your manifestations. Are you in the flow and keeping up with your desires?

Some days will be naturally rewarding and pleasurable, other days less so. Appreciating the peaks and valleys will enable you to sync with your rhythm, raise your vibration and magnify your manifesting skills. Recognising and enjoying the wonderful and fun moments in your life is easy. But it takes skill to climb a mountain, be good at your chosen career, or even navigate emotional hurt.

Peaks and valleys initiate a wave pulse, the vibrational signature of your desire. Running from the valley into the peak will only provide half the information needed to manifest a desire, creating an inferior version. The same goes for running from the peak and trying to create from the valley. You may think, "Who would do that?" But we have been conditioned to structure our lives from this perspective. Think about the following ideas that society holds and perpetuates:

"We must work hard and suffer to get what we want."

"Great art comes from pain and suffering."

"The only way to get past an obstacle is to conquer it."

The trough of the wave allows you to experience the contrast of what you desire, which offers you clarity, resilience, and gratitude for what is coming. It can feel overwhelming; naturally, you don't want to experience the lows. The trough is needed to inspire a path of newness to the peak, and the peak allows the fullest experience of your desires. Be the flow!

Explore the exercises in the masterclass to embody the message and go with the flow.

Conscious Creator Masterclass: Ride Your Wave of Desire

The previous masterclass worked with the principle of vibration and how your emotions and feelings offer a way to align with your soul and desires. This masterclass introduces the idea of universal rhythm and how to ride vibrational waves and go with the flow. The following visualisation gives you an energetic experience of your desires on their way to becoming manifested — a preview of what will likely emerge. This space allows you to clarify and adjust any element for a better experience. Have fun creating!

Visualisation

Find a comfortable place to sit or lie down. Place the *Dancing with Your Rhythm* card at your feet. In your mind, repeat your manifestation name or the word 'dance' nine times. Gently close your eyes. Sense your body and concentrate on your breathing. Follow your breath inward. Hold for five seconds. Breathe out and release all tension. Relax and breathe naturally.

Gently settle your attention and awareness in the middle of your chest to initiate the unfolding of a desire. The vibrational signature of your desire creates a wave that stretches into the universe, stirring the ocean of infinite possibilities. Feel the rhythm of your desire like you are dancing with it. Float in the peak experience of your desire in a beautiful place called 'Summer'. Play with the beauty of your desire; let it merge and expand your consciousness, knowing it will soon turn up in your life.

You begin to ride your wave downwards through the release of 'Autumn'. Feel your desire rushing into the past to create more enhanced versions of it. It will always be with you as a memory in your heart. The wave moves you into the valley, into the shadow of 'Winter'. Something here feels disregarded and unloved, needing to be cleaned up to help you create and be more. These things move out of the shadow. Relief washes over you as you realise these things are part of you and made up of unrealised dreams that you were told to disregard. Collect them up, hug them, and welcome them home. Your wave takes you upwards into new desires and the renewal of 'Spring'. You pick up speed as you create new skills and adventures. Then you are in 'Summer' again, experiencing a desire...

Ride the wave of your desires for at least a minute.

Gently ride your wave back into your heart. Acknowledge where you are and know that each phase of the wave is needed to manifest your dreams. Honour the space and the emotions, be kind to yourself, listen and love every aspect of you. Don't leave any part of you out in the cold, they will be sad and keep knocking, turning up as triggers. Let all of yourself in for your beautiful life.

Take two deep breaths in and out. Wiggle your toes and fingers, stretch your body and open your eyes.

Journal Work

Following the visualisation, jot down or sketch your impressions of each season, exploring the varied elements necessary for manifesting your desires fully.

Summer — Be present with and enjoy your manifested desire.
Autumn — Release and let go to make space for more desires.

Winter — Embrace and love all of you, and clean up anything holding you back.

Spring — Keep planting new seeds of dreams and desires.

Reflections and Actions

Understanding the language of the heart reveals your unique soul beat and how it pulses in rhythm with others, nature, and the universe.

The heart has four needs: *attention*, *affection*, *appreciation*, and *acceptance*. Engaging with the four needs sharpens your intuition and flow, unveiling the heart as a precise instrument resonating with your emotions and feelings. Your heart interprets this information, guiding you towards what needs embracing, allowing, or healing, all the while dancing in tandem with your soul.

Attention encourages you to listen to yourself and be a good listener for others. *Affection* asks you to care for yourself and be kind to others. *Appreciation* is a state of gratitude. Practise self-congratulation, celebrating even minor achievements, and express gratitude to others for their contributions. *Acceptance* entails embracing your authentic self—and the world around you—as they are.

There are lots of activities you could take part in to help embody all of this, such as joining a drum circle, or taking dance lessons — salsa, belly, ballroom, or whatever inspires you. Moving your body in time with music will improve your relationship with your authentic nature. If you are feeling adventurous, you can try ecstatic dance — a free-form dance movement encouraging free expression and release to the rhythm that can lead to trance and a feeling of ecstasy.

18. NOTHING HAPPENS BY CHANCE

Every desire has a story to tell.

To fulfil an authentic, soul-led life, align with the vibe of your soul. Circumstances and experiences recalibrate your frequency. The universe seeks harmony, freeing you to live your best life.

Message

Something has come out of left field that has altered the course of your life. It has been on its way for a while because you have been craving change deep within. This situation confirms what you already know — that a part of your life is transforming. Every cause has an effect. Nothing appears without a purpose. You have done nothing wrong. This situation arrived to let you know a part of you didn't align with your soul's desires. Take a breath and know the answers are coming.

Be open and curious. If you desire a new move, relationship, or job, opportunities will arise to bring them into being. If you want a different outcome to what has happened in the past, you must go about it differently. If you apply the same strategies as before, you will end up with similar results, and these results instigate change.

For example, years ago, I complained to a spiritual teacher about my romantic partners and how I wanted them to be different. She gently asked, "And who is the common denominator in these relationships?" I moved from disbelief and denial to laughter in about twenty seconds, which felt much longer. "Me." I was the common denominator, and if I wanted to change, I had to become clear with my desire and become the person I wanted my partners to be.

No external authority decides if you have been good enough to be rewarded or bad enough to have something taken away. When you recognise a dysfunctional pattern, celebrate your wise ability to see it. Then, be willing to use your new viewpoint to identify any parts that need to be transformed. You can't stop anything that has already manifested, but it can inspire you to create new paths aligned with your soul's truth.

Explore the exercises in the masterclass to embody the message and embrace change.

Conscious Creator Masterclass: Give and Receive in Harmony

The previous masterclass presented the concept of riding the waves of creation while being in the flow of your heart's resonance. This masterclass introduces why creating from higher vibrations is preferable.

Visualisation

Find a comfortable place to sit or lie down. Place the *Nothing Happens by Chance* card at your feet. In your mind, repeat your manifestation name or the word 'certainty' nine times. Gently close your eyes. Sense your body and concentrate on your breathing. Follow your breath inward. Hold for five seconds. Breathe out and release all tension. Relax and breathe naturally.

Reflect on your best qualities: kindness, patience, humility, honesty, compassion, and generosity. Allow all these qualities to rise within you and thank them for all they do for you. Imagine they all merge and spiral into your heart. The spiral then spins the opposite way, swirling outward. You begin to see your best qualities in everyone around you. Spiral your best qualities to them. If they are in the vibrational vicinity to tune in to your beautiful vibes, they will be inspired to move into higher vibrations. Imagine that your spiral encourages all to have what they need.

You are creating a change in yourself and others, helping yourself and others realise that nothing happens by chance. When you deliberately focus on your best qualities, solutions and answers will arrive. Whatever has taken you by surprise, invite it to be with you. You feel joyous and calm. Spend a couple of minutes gently floating with your 'surprise' to gain any information it has to share.

Gently bring your attention to your physical body. Breathe the solutions into your body, wiggle your toes and fingers, stretch your body, and open your eyes.

Journal Work

After the visualisation, write or draw your best qualities and how you apply them. The more you work with the energy, the more you will recognise it. Write or draw anything that may have come to you. This helps you create a path for future solutions to arrive.

Reflections and Actions
Everyone is a creator, but what type of creator are you? Read the descriptions below and determine what type of creator you are now, and what type you would like to be. With awareness and knowledge of the different creator levels, you can become a powerful creator that will bring consistent results.

Unaware Creator (stuck-in-the-box thinking)
The unaware creator is precisely that — unaware that familiar and conditioned ideas, beliefs, and patterns are orchestrating how they will experience life. Unaware creation feels awful because we don't know what is coming or what we've done to cause it. They believe things are happening to them and can't change the outcome. To awaken to the level of an aware creator, realise that you may not be able to change the circumstances. However, you can change the way you react and respond.

Aware Creator (thinking outside the box)
The aware creator has concluded that they create how they will experience life. The vibrations and frequencies they send out attract things into their life. They know life is happening from them and work with this knowledge to create a better life. You can have, do, or be anything you desire. If you want to transition to a passion creator, intend for your manifestations to create better ways for all of us to live instead of filling a void or satisfying a craving.

Passion Creator (there is no box)

The passion creator knows that anything is possible. This may seem like a miracle to others, but the passion creator lives their desires, regardless of whether or not anyone else can see them. They become their passions and strive to create new ways to enrich the lives of humans, animals, and nature. To be a passion creator, turn inward and get to know yourself, your thoughts, and vibrations. Then, adjust any imbalances to align with your heart and soul. Practise coming back home to your heart every day. Go to the information for *Heartfulness* and *Meditation* cards to learn how to harmonise your energy and move into your balanced heart.

19. THE HARMONY OF CONTRAST

The interplay of light and shadow.

A desire arrives in your awareness with all its nuances. The light becomes brighter because of the darkness. Neither is right or wrong. All paradoxes can be resolved.

Message

You keep attracting the opposite of your desire and are ready to give up on the notion that you can direct and create desires. But wait, there is more. The saying "opposites attract" is true. Take a breath. All is well, so let's delve into the principle of polarity.

Every dream or desire has two sides — what you want and what you fear. Consider a pole with 'I want to be well' on one end and 'I don't want to be sick' on the other. If your attention leans towards fearing sickness, you emit the vibration of sickness rather than wellness. Similar dualities exist, such as 'I want financial security' versus 'I fear lack of money' and 'I desire a relationship' versus 'I dread being alone'.

You may believe you are thinking about something you desire, but your attention is on the opposite because you don't want to experience it — which, of course, brings it into your experience. Your inner guidance can tell which pole you are leaning towards. Does your heart sing or shrink when you think or speak of your desire? Do you feel excited or anxious? The feelings may be subtle, but they are there. Pause for a moment and tune in. Check out the *Emotions* card for extra information.

When you tune in to a statement that fills you with joy, note it and incorporate it into your thoughts or find similar uplifting statements. Conversely, if you express negative sentiments such as, "I never want to go through that," or, "I wish it was different," pause and assess your emotional state. Contrasts in our reality are inevitable and serve as opportunities for growth. Embracing this contrast allows you to ask more expansive questions, leading to greater desires for personal and collective betterment.

Explore the exercises in the masterclass to embody the message and feel your way through contrast into harmony.

Conscious Creator Masterclass: Becoming Harmony

The previous masterclass presented why creating from higher vibrations is preferable. This masterclass introduces the concept that you need contrast to create new ideas and desires. It creates a tension that reveals a need for a solution.

Visualisation

Find a comfortable place to sit down. Place *The Harmony of Contrast* card at your feet with your hands on your knees. In your mind, repeat your manifestation name or the word 'harmonise' nine times. Gently close your eyes. Sense your body and concentrate on your breathing.

Float inward on your breath and go with it to your heart. Place your hands on your heart and enter the diamond temple at the centre of your heart. Then, place your hands on your lap. As you gently float towards the centre of your diamond, the colours of the rainbow fill the space. As you move through each colour, allow it to inspire deeper information about your likes and dislikes, unique to that colour. Float through each colour, red, orange, yellow, green, blue, and purple. From purple, you drift into a bright, white light. You can sense wisdom pouring into your awareness, and you understand the colours of the rainbow are simply different expressions of white light. The journey through the colours has expanded your understanding and defined your desires.

A massive pot of gold manifests at the centre of your diamond. You feel an urge to climb in and giggle as you do. You are the pot of gold and the rainbow shining in all directions. Allow your light to shine into the hearts of all and the heart of the universe, filling them with energy, happiness, intelligence, friendship, gentleness, and beauty.

Float in this space for at least a minute, shining your light in absolute bliss.

When you feel ready, allow the wisdom of contrasting colours to flow as you float through your diamond into your heart. Take a deep breath and be present in all the contrasting beautiful colours that are your physical body. Open your eyes to the beauty of diversity.

Journal Work

After the visualisation, write or draw about your journey through the colours of the rainbow. What did each colour reveal about your preferences, dislikes, and desires? Describe your experience of climbing into the pot of gold through writing or illustrating. How did it feel? Reflect on the sensation of shining your light into the hearts of others and the universe. What impact did this have on you? Reflect on the beauty of diversity in your life. What are you grateful for? How can this sense of gratitude help you maintain bliss and harmony in your daily life?

Reflections and Actions

Contrast is an impactful design concept. It brings exciting elements to a bland space. If you feel that your life has stalled or lacks novelty, contrast will quickly and simply inject something new into your life. Now that you know this is a part of the creation process, you can use it to explore opposites and experiment with different ideas. Joining a debate team can help you explore and experiment with different perspectives. Or you could explore an art class to learn about the role of contrast in bringing an image to life.

Your dreams and desires exist beyond your comfort zone. Be open to receiving ideas that are outside your comfort zone. You can transcend any contrast and become more resilient. One suggestion is to learn how to survive in the wild or bush; nature is our best teacher for adapting and adjusting to any situation.

20. DIVINE FEMININE

Embrace your inner moon.

Honour the moon goddess, the divine feminine within all humans. Across cycles, the Maiden, Mother, and Crone cast moonlit rays, nurturing your inner desires.

Message

Creative, joyous fun is on its way through deepening a relationship or reconciliation with a woman, a group of women, or the essence of femininity. You will also discover or reconnect with the goddess within, who will shine her silvery moonlight on your most profound dreams, hidden in your shadow, because you are ready to see and realise them.

Our deepest, secret passions can often feel so impossible to manifest that we hide them. The Divine Feminine wants you to know she has caught and embraced your dreams. She has been nurturing them, but now she hands them back because you are ready to bring them into being. If you don't feel ready, plant the idea in your fertile mind. You will know when to allow them to grow or transform into new dreams.

The trinity of Maiden, Mother, and Crone (the triple goddess) signifies the feminine principles of creation. The Divine Feminine is within us all, regardless of gender. Each trinity aspect must be realised, lived, and embodied to complete a chapter of your life successfully. The Maiden brings passion and excitement to light up your potential. The Mother showers your inner child with unconditional love so you can nurture your desires into ideas that thrive. The Crone gifts certainty and confidence to unleash your bold wisdom to accept, forgive, and understand endings.

Explore the exercises in the masterclass to embody the message and shine a light on your deepest desires.

Conscious Creator Masterclass: Experiencing your Divine Feminine

The previous masterclass discussed the concept that contrast is needed to create new ideas and desires. This masterclass introduces the Divine Feminine — the creating, receptive principle.

Visualisation
Find a comfortable place to sit down. Place the *Divine Feminine* card at your feet. In your mind, repeat your manifestation name or the word 'moon' nine times. Gently close your eyes. Sense your body and concentrate on your breathing. Focus on the middle of your chest and relax into your heart, the gateway to the Divine Feminine.

A beautiful moon enters your space. It shines a magical silver light into your depths and all around you. Your inner goddess emerges from the darkness and, with a flick of her wrist, creates a magical, beautiful temple filled with your deepest treasures. She invites you into the temple to walk among a treasure-trove of ideas, possibilities, thought experiments, childhood dreams, and fascinations. A sense of wonderment and relief washes over you as you reunite with your creative potential. Let this energy permeate every part of you.

Give birth to all your creations; let them see the light of day as you bask in loving feminine energy. Float in this space for at least a minute.

When you feel ready, focus on your breath and vow that your dreams and desires will always be in the light. Even if you don't know how they will manifest, let them be with you. Allow your Maiden, Mother, and Crone to come together and breathe your Divine Feminine energy into your creations and your body. Wiggle your toes and fingers. Then, stretch your body and open your eyes.

Journal Work

After the visualisation, write or draw the inner treasures you saw in your temple. Go through each one and decide if you still desire it or if it has stirred new, clarified desires. Your life is yours to create so don't allow your deepest desires to wither away in the dark. Let them shine.

Reflections and Actions

A deeper connection and communication with your Divine Feminine initiates ideas and creation from your inner expression, instead of other people's manifestations. Learn to listen and trust your inner thoughts and ideas and keep them to yourself until you are ready to birth them.

Each day, be open to inspired actions that will support and bring your inner gold into the physical world.

Spend time with women of all ages and open your mind to hear their unique approaches to life.

Research Moon Astrology to discover your Moon sign. It will help you understand your inner emotional landscape.

Tune in to the lunar cycle to create new ideas at the new moon and at the full moon, shine a light on your manifestations and celebrate them. Check out the *Moon Illumination* card for a way to measure and track your desires and manifestations.

21. DIVINE MASCULINE

Embrace your inner sun.

Honour the sun god, the divine masculine within all humans. Each day, the Warrior, Father, and Sage beam life-affirming sunrays, nurturing and championing your desires into reality.

Message

You feel a deep need to respect your ideas and give them a way to manifest. Inspired action will encourage you to start that project, enterprise, or adventure. A relationship with a man, a group of men, or the masculine principle will give you the courage and discipline to step into your power. You've got this! You will also discover or reconnect with your inner god, whose golden sunlight will light the path of your dreams and help them manifest.

When a dream is deeply personal, it can feel safer to keep it in your mind, but the dream wants to be realised as much as you want to experience it. The Divine Masculine has an energetic hand on your back. It is gently, lovingly pushing you forwards into your inner strengths so you can be the leader of your thoughts and emotions. You are learning to stand your ground and regain your self-respect.

The trinity of Warrior, Father, and Sage signifies the masculine principles of action. The Divine Masculine is within us all, regardless of gender. Each part of the trinity helps you to understand and complete a chapter of your life. The Warrior brings curiosity to gather experience and explore new horizons, breaking through old limitations and finding his centre. The Father shows love by establishing structures that support and protect the creative element. The Sage no longer needs recognition through performance and success; instead, he guides all to their integrity and wisdom. He feels free to contribute beauty and inner purpose for the greater good.

Explore the exercises in the masterclass to embody the message and shine a light on your courage and vulnerability, which will assist you in building innovative dreams and pathways.

Conscious Creator Masterclass: Experiencing your Divine Masculine

The previous masterclass introduced the Divine Feminine principle, which is the part of us that receives the ideas for creation. This masterclass works with the concept of the Divine Masculine, the manifesting, giving principle.

Visualisation

Find a comfortable place to sit down. Place the *Divine Masculine* card at your feet. In your mind, repeat your manifestation name or the word 'sun' nine times. Gently close your eyes. Sense your body and concentrate on your breathing. Focus on your solar plexus and relax into your gut, the pathway to the Divine Masculine.

A beautiful sun enters your space. It shines a magical golden light into your depths, fuelling your inner fire to create a beautiful violet and red glow around you. The inner is becoming the outer. Your inner god emerges from the fire. He invites you to follow him through the fire to a sun temple. The fire burns away anything holding you back, and as you enter the temple, you experience all your deepest desires manifested. A sense of amazement and relief washes over as you realise you will do what you set out to do. You have a new-found confidence in forming any actions required to manifest your ideas.

Allow your inner fire to enlighten and warm your inner masculine. Feel old masks melting away and let your self-esteem and confidence shine through for all to see and be inspired by. Bask in the energy of engagement and accomplishment for at least a minute.

When you feel ready, focus on your breath. Thank the sun for the transforming fire that inspired a direct connection with your inner creator. Allow your divine masculine experience to be with you as you breathe action into your body. Wiggle your toes and fingers. Then, stretch your body and open your eyes.

Journal Work

After the visualisation, write or draw the desires you saw manifesting in your life. Go through each one and decide if it was what you thought it would be or feel like. This allows you to clarify and change your desires. Your life is yours to create; don't allow your perfectionism to stop you from shining your light. You can't get it wrong!

Reflections and Actions
Thank the Sun for illuminating all your manifested ideas and creations, as well as for inspiring actions that encourage you to be more inventive and generous.

Read autobiographies of famous men that impress you.

Have your astrology chart prepared to understand all the characteristics that flow through your sun sign (also known as your zodiac sign).

Believe you have within you something that only you can manifest for the improvement of your life and others. Create a vision for your community, country, or the world. You will require a vision bigger than your comfort zone to make a difference. Invoke your inner strength: you can do this.

22. SACRED UNION

Uniting the Divine Masculine and Feminine.

Our hearts and minds desire unity with ourselves and others. This starts by compassionately acknowledging any pain, then embracing it without judgement, and creating a space of unconditional love for your soul's desires to flourish.

Message

Here is a loving invitation to deepen your inner connections and treat yourself as Earth's most precious person. The more you love and embrace yourself, the easier it is to love and embrace others. Every part of you wants to be loved and take part in the eternal cosmic love affair between the masculine and feminine, physical and non-physical, god and goddess, matter and spirit. When you bring these two sides of yourself together, you will birth new spiritual, emotional, and physical manifestations.

The Divine Masculine and Feminine describe a dance of archetypal polarities within each person, regardless of gender. Masculine energy is giving, logical, analytical, and external.

Feminine energy is receptive, intuitive, creative, and internal. The Divine Feminine draws on the moon's wisdom, connecting to our inner world to delve into all that is mysterious and undefined, forming the thoughts and seeds for the masculine to manifest. The Divine Masculine draws on the movement and knowledge of the sun, connecting to our outer world and allowing all things from our inner selves to be brought into the light to grow and manifest into the physical.

Look at the card's image. Direct your attention to the feminine water of life being stirred under the couple. The geometric shapes and hearts are ideas being birthed. On your exhale, imagine an explosion of beautiful blue, purple, and red shapes. These are the beginnings of what you will manifest into reality. You have just felt a sacred union creating and making newness. Over the next few days, take note of new solutions and creative ideas dropping into your mind and an incredible physical creation that will bring you much joy.

Explore the exercises in the masterclass to embody the message and learn from the love that the Divine Masculine and Feminine have for each other.

Conscious Creator Masterclass: The Union of Your Inner Polarities

The previous masterclass presented the concept of the Divine Masculine, the manifesting, giving principle. This masterclass introduces how to bring together the contrast within yourself, known as the divine masculine and feminine principles.

Visualisation

Find a comfortable place to sit down. Put the *Sacred Union* card between your feet to activate and ground the energy of togetherness. Place your hands on your lap. In your mind, repeat your manifestation name or the word 'unite' nine times. Gently close your eyes. Sense your body and concentrate on your breathing. Follow your breath inward. Hold for five seconds. Breathe out and release all tension. Relax and breathe naturally.

Raise your right hand in front of you with your palm facing upwards. Focus on your right hand bringing forth your representation of the masculine. Sense his energy swirling around your hand. Ask him how he feels and what he wants to share with you. Then, ask him what he needs to be whole and complete. Listen with an open heart. Then imagine a waterfall of liquid gold light washing over him until he feels balanced and loved. Place your right hand in your lap.

Raise your left hand in front of you with your palm facing upwards. Focus on your left hand bringing forth your representation of the feminine. Sense her energy swirling around your hand. Ask her how she feels and what she wants to share with you. Then, ask her what she needs to be whole and complete. Listen with an open heart. Then imagine a waterfall of liquid silver light washing over her until she feels balanced and loved. Place your left hand in your lap.

Now, bring both hands together over your heart and imagine both representations living together in your heart as equal partners. You will now attract people and circumstances that vibrate in wholeness. You don't need anything from each other. Instead, you will encourage each other to be everything you can be. This is freedom.

Creating a sacred union within you sends vibrations of unconditional love into the world and universe, bringing variations of unconditional love back to you. Take two deep breaths in and out. Wiggle your toes and fingers, stretch your body, and open your eyes.

Journal Work

After the visualisation, write or draw how the masculine and feminine parts of you felt. Did they manifest as a person, animal, or symbol? Then, write or draw how it felt to have both aspects living in your heart. Did they merge to create something new?

Reflections and Actions

Whether you have a partner or are self-partnering, the following exercises can enhance sacred union.

- Have a massage/couples massage or learn to massage yourself.
- Try eye gazing by standing in front of a mirror and look yourself in the eyes for five minutes. Then record your experiences and feelings. With your partner spend five minutes gazing into each other's eyes then discuss with each other what it felt like.
- Explore tantric techniques, which focus on connecting deeply through breath, touch, and energy exchange.

Research yoga. The word 'yoga' means union and is an ancient system that offers wisdom, techniques, and practices to support physical, mental, and spiritual wellbeing. It's more than just getting into postures. To learn more about the tradition, I suggest reading *The Autobiography of a Yogi* by Paramahansa Yogananda.

23. ABUNDANCE

Feel everlasting prosperity.

You are always plentiful in something because there are many forms of abundance. When you let go of trying to be abundant, you will quickly tune in to what reflects your true nature and be open to acting on that.

Message

A stream of abundance is coming to you; open your heart and mind to receive it. It may manifest differently to what you expect. But it will create a sense of wealth and freedom.

The word 'abundance' translates from the Latin *abundantia* and means 'overflowing'. What areas of your life do you feel this overflowing — knowledge, empathy, listening, love, family, or relationships? Developing a more profound sense of abundance begins with discovering how much you already have and what you can share with others to improve your and their lives.

Be like the people in the card's image who are ready to receive the abundance flowing towards them. If they had their backs to the abundance, do you think it would come to them or flow straight past them? You attract what you are. You may be more comfortable giving, but to complete the abundance cycle of manifestation, you must allow yourself to receive as easily as you give. Then, you will have many things to give without feeling a lack of energy or resources. To give is to receive, and to receive is to give.

Explore the exercises in the masterclass to embody the message and feel your way into abundance.

Conscious Creator Masterclass: Discover Your Abundance

The previous masterclass presented how to bring together the contrast of divine masculine and feminine principles within yourself. This masterclass introduces the concept of abundant thinking to bring more into your life.

Visualisation

Sitting down, place your hands on your lap face up, with the *Abundance* card between your feet. In your mind, repeat your manifestation name or the word 'plenty' nine times. Close your eyes softly and tenderly. Focus on the middle of your chest and imagine floating on waves of crystal white light to your inner temple. It is so bright, beautiful, and inviting.

Your manifestation name or the word 'plenty' materialises over the top of the entrance. Float up the stairs and enter your temple. An angel greets you, takes you by your hands and transports you to a beautiful expanse of green grass surrounded by tall trees. The angel whispers into your ear: "Listen with your heart. Open your heart to receive." You sense the strong vibrations flowing from the grass and trees. You honour them by experiencing the wisdom and abundance of the earth. Your angel directs you to lie on the grass and take deep, slow breaths.

On the next deep inhale, say, "I am who I am." As you breathe out, say, "I am love." Take another deep breath and say, "I receive abundance." As you exhale say, "I give abundance." Take one more deep breath and say, "I am abundance," and as you exhale say, "You are abundance." Feel your whole body soften and relax as you melt into the grass and wisdom of Mother Earth. You are a living cell in her body. Allow her to embrace you in her emerald green light. Allow her unconditional support to open ways of birthing new creations into physical form. Float in the healing green light of creation and stay here for at least a minute.

Your angel takes you by your hands again and transports you back to the entrance of your temple. Thank them as they fly away. Like the image, they are a part of your inner temple, shining abundance, love, and wisdom in every moment for you to connect with. You see the people in the image and realise they are you. Excitedly, you float towards them on the waves of crystal white light. The three aspects of giving, receiving, and abundance merge into one. You feel an expanded prosperity and a strong knowledge that the rest of your life will be comfortable and pleasing. Breathe into your glorious, physical body. Come back to the here and now. Wiggle your toes and fingers, stretch your body, and open your eyes to a wealth of abundance around you.

Journal Work

After the visualisation, write or draw what abundance feels and looks like to you. Then, write or draw how you think Mother Earth works with us to create abundance. Committing this to paper or a device anchors the intention and informs the universe and Mother Earth that you are ready for greater abundance to create a better world for her, you, and all.

Reflections and Actions

Ask yourself what abundance brings to you. Is it a feeling of safety, that your needs are being met, or having lots of family and friends? Become clear about what that means for you. Focus on where you feel abundant in your life now, and you will create more variations of abundant thinking that attract yet more abundance.

Be gentle with yourself and develop self-compassion. Being hard on yourself will limit abundance. When you catch yourself holding limiting beliefs, stop, breathe, drop your shoulders, relax your jaw, and be compassionate. You are doing the best you can; tomorrow, you will know more and do your best then.

Learn something new. Ignite your curiosity about others and the world around you. Begin by learning the backstory of both a famous person you admire and someone who annoys you. It is fascinating to learn what shaped a person to become who they are today, and it will help you understand something about yourself that expands your abundance mentality.

24. INNOVATION

Combine old and new ideas.

You have something extraordinary and innovative to offer the world. It could be your smile, which makes someone's day, or an answer to pollution. Everything is needed to grow into a new way of co-creating with ourselves and the universe.

Message

New ideas and novel solutions are about to drop into your awareness. Inspired action will emerge from these insights and show how to simplify any area of your life. The energy of innovation fosters continuous improvement in your life. It gently propels you forwards into more fabulous experiences of your desires.

Your life's energy is occupied with creation, growth, and change, so, in time, you will outgrow what you thought you couldn't live without. New, diverse experiences and people will open you to ideas and things you didn't even know you wanted but now are curious and excited about manifesting and engaging in.

Be open to new ways of kindness, curiosity, and dreaming big dreams. If life feels like it has stalled and no innovations are coming or happening, be mindful that sometimes it takes a while to formulate an idea and for the components to come together. Know that a lot is happening behind the scenes of your everyday life, even if you can't see it. Learn to focus on what you already have in your life and find gratitude. Before you know it, life will take off again. Give it time for seeds to grow. You are the inspiration and innovator of your life.

Explore the exercises in the masterclass to embody the message and start a sense of improvement.

Conscious Creator Masterclass: Making the Old into New

The previous masterclass introduced the concept of manifesting prosperity through receiving and giving abundance. This masterclass expands on the concept that innovation involves receiving ideas for new solutions and contributing something novel to the world through your creations and manifestations.

Visualisation
Find a comfortable place to sit or lie down. Place the *Innovation* card at your feet. In your mind, repeat your manifestation name or the word 'fresh' nine times. Close your eyes softly and tenderly. Focus on the middle of your chest and imagine walking on a magical path leading to your heart and inner landscape. Concentrate all your attention inward and take four deep, slow breaths.

Focus on a deep longing within your soul. What aspect of your life do you wish to enhance or develop further? Invite your soul to reveal the sensations and images associated with this desire. Allow yourself to gently explore and visualise your expanded self, envisioning any areas you wish to refine. From this deep wisdom arises an innovative mandala, reflecting the imagery of the card. Visualise this mandala forming beneath you, providing a solid foundation for growth. Now, shift your attention to the lotus flower suspended above the mandala, floating gracefully above your head.

As you focus on the lotus, your mind merges with it, and a portal to innovation opens for you to explore. Enter it and feel the excitement of change as the energy of innovation allows you to feel sensations and see images, understanding that something new and improved is forming in your life. You are building a bridge connecting your imagination with practicality, bringing ideas to life that will manifest and transform your life, work, and how you interact with yourself and others.

Stay in this revolutionary space for at least one minute. Imagine your attention has manifested into a bright, inspiring light and allow it to move through the portal into the lotus. Allow your light to flow effortlessly from the lotus, streaming down through the crown of your head, coursing through your body, and extending out through the soles of your feet, merging with the mandala below. You are grounding your experiences, which will soon manifest into your awareness.

Take two deep, slow breaths and navigate your awareness to the here and now. Open your eyes and re-enter your innovative physical life.

Journal Work

After the visualisation, write about or draw at least one new idea you experienced. If you can't recall a new idea, write or draw how you would like to improve one area of your life. Committing your thoughts to paper or on a device plants the ideas into your foundation mandala, giving them a platform to grow from and springboard into your life.

Reflections and Actions

Recall something you did that other people tried to dissuade you from doing. You knew it would be right for you, and it worked well. Write or draw about this experience and then add how that situation empowered you.

Nudge your mind towards new ways of living — tomorrow, rise from the other side of the bed, or change up your normal routine. Be gentle to your body as you make changes; you are retraining body memory.

The more times you try new things, the easier it will become. Begin by activating the belief that you are safe and can try new things. Place both hands at your solar plexus and breathe the white light of innovation from the card image in and out of your belly button. You will build a rock-solid foundation that you can grow from. You are esteeming yourself, realising that trying new things is joyous and fun, and this dramatically outweighs any apprehension.

25. Visionary

Seeing the path of most allowance.

To have a vision is to dream big and know it is possible. Not everyone will share your view, so keep it to yourself until you are unquestionably confident, for certainty is your faith.

Message

You are a visionary, but sometimes you doubt yourself and do not believe something is true until others see it. Have confidence in your visions; you are the only one who can. A visionary knows that an inner dream will come to be. It may not happen quite as you expect, but variations of it will manifest for you to enjoy and expand upon.

A vision begins inside of you, in your imagination and your dreams, and will grab all the higher possibilities to create vivid scenarios, compelling you to nurture them into reality. Your soul witnesses all from a higher perspective and revels in the boundless, creative imagination of your visions. Everything in this world was first a dream that someone thought into existence. The building blocks that make everything in your world are within you. Realise your dreams by activating your inner visionary.

It is your job to know your dreams fully and intimately. Connect to your dreams by immersing yourself into the vision and then experiencing them directly through all your senses — what does it look like, sound like, feel like?

Explore the exercises in the masterclass to embody the message and create a higher viewing platform of your life.

Conscious Creator Masterclass: Moving a Vision from the Inner to Outer Self

The previous masterclass introduced the concept of innovation: receiving ideas will provide solutions that will give something new to the world through your creations and manifestations. This masterclass opens your mind and heart to your soul possibilities and the bigger picture of your dreams and desires.

Visualisation

Find a comfortable place to sit, hold the *Visionary* card gently in your hands. In your mind, repeat your manifestation name or the word 'prophet' nine times. Bring to your mind a dream that makes your heart smile. Allow it to journey with you. Close your eyes softly and tenderly. Concentrate all your attention inward and take four deep, slow breaths as you imagine walking on a magical path leading to your heart and inner landscape.

While still absorbed in your internal space, gently open your eyes and focus on the card in your hands. Take four deep, slow breaths. Now, shift a part of your inward attention to your outside world by directing your gaze at something around you within two metres. Take four deep and slow breaths. Now, softly move more of your inner attention to the outside world by gazing at a point of convergence, a meeting place like the horizon in the image. This brings all possibilities of your vision together. Take four deep, slow breaths.

Now, close your eyes again and imagine that point of convergence as a ball of light. Expand that ball of light to embrace the earth. Feel your dream forming. Soon, it will enter your life in varied and beautifully satisfying ways. Expand your ball of light and see it reaching out into the infinite creative space of the universe, like electrical impulses expanding and creating new life and ideas. Experience your dream from this expanded view and float in the possibilities of what it can become.

Breathe deeply and stay here for as long as you like, at least thirty seconds. When you are ready, draw your awareness back to the point of convergence and open your eyes. Re-orient your consciousness by gazing at something around you, within two metres. Take two deep, slow breaths while fully concentrating on the *Visionary* card in your hands. What do you see? How do you feel? Take two more deep, slow breaths and return to waking consciousness.

Journal Work

Write or draw about the expanded perception of the dream you experienced in the visualisation. Did you learn anything new, or why you desire something? This enquiry will create a clearer picture to bring into reality. Then, write or draw a list of big dreams and desires you can play with next time you do the visualisation. Go wild! Let your visionary dream big.

Reflections and Actions

Activating your imagination will open your mind and heart to your greatest potential. Take just ten minutes a day to play and daydream.

Try this exercise: Imagine you are a character in an adventure movie. What would be your story? Write or draw a one-page outline of your movie script. If you get stuck, think about the movies or stories that have impacted you. Be your own hero/heroine.

Cultivate a visionary mindset by nurturing your curiosity about the world. Open your mind to new ideas, and practise big-picture thinking. The details will fill in over time. For the moment, expand your desires and allow space for you to grow into.

Question assumptions, especially the ones in your mind, and believe that you have the power to sculpt the future.

26. WOULDN'T IT BE LOVELY

Sow dreams and desires in your mind's garden.

Dream big and allow desires to arise in your higher mind, heart, and every cell within your body. Lovingly nurture them into manifestation by entrusting them to the journey of creation.

Message

Allow yourself to wander into a 'wouldn't it be lovely' scenario and plant seeds of fantastic notions into the garden of your mind. Let loose. Dream your wildest desires. No more holding back; proceed with creation. The playing field of life is unlimited and loving.

You are an unlimited, loving, and wondrous part of creation. You are perfect — right here, right now. You are different and, therefore, think differently from last week, last year, last decade, yet you will always be you. The events and experiences in your life will grow in meaning as your consciousness expands. You came here to honour the physical process of creation, to become more of the joy and wonderment that you are.

Everything you say and do becomes true for you and is the platform on which you build your life. Are you keeping up with your life and all you want to create? Or are you holding yourself back with 'what-if's or 'but's? Like most of us, you have been holding your dreams close to your heart to keep them safe. However, they yearn to live.

Take a moment and a deep breath ... in and out. Then, imagine you breathe into your heart. Open the door to your heart and let loose your dreams. You will feel better, softer, and easier. Now, you don't have to protect or justify your deepest desires. By letting them go, they will find their way back to you as a physical manifestation. Isn't that exciting? Go for it and dream up the most spectacular life ever.

Explore the exercises in the masterclass to embody the message and anchor your desires into the earth.

Conscious Creator Masterclass: Planting Your Desires

The previous masterclass introduced the possibilities and bigger picture of your dreams and desires. You are bringing your dreams to life through your imagination. This masterclass introduces the concept of planting your desires into the earth, metaphorically and literally. You are grounding yourself and your dreams.

Visualisation

Find a comfortable place to sit down. Place your hands on your lap face up, with the *Wouldn't It Be Lovely* card at your feet. In your mind, repeat your manifestation name or the word 'dream' nine times. Close your eyes softly and tenderly. Then imagine floating on magical blue waves. You are relaxed and calm. Breathe deeply as the blue waves take you deep into your purple heart of wisdom and insight.

Hues of purple and blue swirl all around you. Among the swirling light, you can feel desires and dreams, old and new, excitedly dancing. You have released them from your mind to be planted and become a foundation. They have begun a new journey of growth and potential, which has made space for you to create more dreams and desires, to be the creator you are.

You and your heart are beating in time with your dreams and desires. Feel your heart pulsing, throbbing, vibrating as it crafts a sphere of amethyst crystal that contains all your dreams and desires. Hold this sphere in your hands and peer inside. You can see yourself living all your deepest longings. They are here and possible.

Bring to your mind the idea that you want to see a rainbow, look into your sphere, and see yourself standing under a rainbow. Now, bring to your mind something you would like to experience in the next few days. Look into your sphere and see yourself living it. Imagine you can really feel it.

Gently let go of your sphere and watch it float downwards on waves of purple and blue to be planted into the waiting arms of Mother Earth. She catches your sphere and draws it into the earth, planting your seed and nurturing, feeding, and loving it.

Trust and know your seed is growing, and soon it will break through the surface of the earth and manifest physically. Be open to all possibilities, let go of any outcomes, and let it all go. It will happen.

Planting your dreams and desires has given them space to grow. Changes will be made instantaneously in your sphere whenever you clarify or adjust them. When your life inspires new desires, they will immediately enter your sphere and grow. Revel in this beautiful garden of dreams that you have planted.

Feel yourself gently floating from your purple heart on the waves of blue towards your physical life. When you are ready, take two deep, slow breaths and drift into your physical body. Wiggle and stretch your body and open your eyes.

Journal Work

After the visualisation, write or draw about any dreams or desires you saw yourself living in your sphere. Now that you have seen yourself living them, would you like to make any adjustments? If so, write or draw your adjustments. Has this experience inspired any new desires? If so, write or draw about them. Add them to your new moon list (see the *Moon Illumination* card).

Reflections and Actions: Create a Dream-Seed Ball

The following exercise is based on a Japanese practice called *tsuchi dango*, meaning 'earth dumpling'. A Japanese microbiologist and farmer, Masanobu Fukuoka (1913–2008), reintroduced the idea of a seed ball or seed dumpling in 1938. The following is an adaptation of this technique to plant your dreams and desires.

Ingredients
- A small amount of clay
- A small amount of potting mix or quality soil
- Seeds. Choose seeds that are suitable for the area, climate, and season you are in — e.g., indigenous wildflowers, herbs, or trees
- Pen and a small piece of paper to write your desire. Paper size should be approx. 3cm x 1cm or 1.25 x 0.5 inches
- Egg carton or box lined with newspaper to dry your seed ball

Instructions
1. Write your desire on a piece of paper.
2. Take a small piece of clay, about the size of a tablespoon.
3. Roll your clay into a ball.
4. Use your thumb to make a hollow in your clay. It will look like a mini bowl.
5. Place your paper message in the bottom.
6. Add a small pinch of potting mix or soil on top of the paper.
7. Add one or two seeds.
8. Pinch the clay closed again, so the seeds can't fall out and roll into a ball.
9. Place in the egg carton or box to dry for about 24–48 hours.

Seed balls are best planted in spring or autumn. When the time feels right, take your ball and toss it into your garden or a park, or you may feel directed to place it in a specific place. Please gain permission if needed.

Once you have done this, it is time to metaphorically let go of your desire and allow it to germinate and grow. Trust that Mother

Earth will care for your seed. As it grows, inspire yourself to take actions that help grow your desire into reality.

Just like you, the energy of a seed is limitless. It can power its own growth and desire.

27. THE PRE-ARRANGEMENT OF FREE WILL

The destiny of choice.

Your soul's free will chose topics of special interest to explore in this life, often considered destiny. When your personality explores these topics, an excited inward smile prevails and a purpose will unfold. You can choose to follow this or go down another path.

Message

You are refining your inner creator skills and beginning to know your worth, hone your talents, and play to your strengths. Think of yourself as an artist — your life comprises many paintings simultaneously in progress. Everything you create are brush strokes on your life's masterpieces. Your soul created the topics for your masterpieces, and when you and your soul's purpose align, your highest will opens the possibility that all is possible.

The duality of life allows us to choose different perspectives and paths to follow. These choices shape our experiences and help us understand our beliefs and aspirations. To bring about change, use your free will to select new perspectives or paths to explore. Through experiencing these choices, you will determine whether to continue on the same path or seek something new. There are various ways to navigate life, and listening to your inner soul's voice will help you select the pathways to your dreams and desires. Your purpose has always been with you as the actions you take every day. You may call it your values. Applications in life may change, but the essence will be the same. Can you see a predominant theme in your life?

Your soul's free will has your best interests at heart. Let go and allow it to direct you through your intuition. Your soul—just like the universe—learns and expands from all your experiences. When you and your soul flow in unison, your direction becomes clearer. Use your free will to navigate towards your preferred version of anything.

Explore the exercises in the masterclass to embody the message and accept free will.

Conscious Creator Masterclass: Choosing Is Your Superpower

The previous masterclass introduced the wonderment of possibilities for your dreams and desires as you plant them in the earth. This masterclass introduces your ability to choose your desires from a conscious place. When you inadvertently choose from your unconscious, the unknown aspects of yourself make the choices. These choices make it feel as if you have no choice.

Visualisation

Find a comfortable place to sit down. Place *The Prearrangement of Free Will* card at your feet. In your mind, repeat your manifestation name or the word 'freedom' nine times. Gently close your eyes. Sense your body and concentrate on your breathing. Take your focus to the middle of your chest. Breathe into your energetic heart. It grows and expands until it surrounds you in profound love and boundless visions.

Imagine floating in your heart space, surrounded by secret heart wisdom. A shimmering green and pink light surrounds you. You are safe to let go and just be. Here, you bask in the bliss beyond roles and labels. There is no one you need to be and nothing you need to do; there is just you to be. You are entirely free. Feel how amazing it feels to be at peace with yourself and the world around you.

You can choose to feel however you want to. Your emotional experience is everything within yourself. Just for now, imagine you sink deeper into your heart and surrender to the will of your soul. As you relinquish, your soul connection becomes clearer, and a higher meaning of your life flows into your being. And just like the image, feel your passion rise as your soul's spirit emanates from your being and begins to form as a clear destiny, filled with many dreams and desires.

Bask in the energy of your empowerment to choose how you want to feel and where you direct your energy — this is what your future is made of. All is well. You are a powerful, serene person who accepts yourself and others with love. Relax, let go and float in the bliss of co-creating with your soul for at least a minute.

When you feel ready, breathe in the green and pink shimmering light. Your expanded heart draws closer to you, moving into your body along with all you have collected and experienced. You are home. Focus on your breath. Wiggle your toes and fingers. Then stretch your body and open your eyes to a new Earth.

Journal Work

Reflect on your life. Write or draw about what you and your soul have experienced in this life. What do you love? What makes you smile, and what gets you out of bed without setting an alarm? Write or draw any answers to these questions.

Reflections and Actions

Here are some movies about free will and self-determination: *Groundhog Day* (1993), *The Truman Show* (1998), and *Mr. Nobody* (2009).

When you reach for a snack, pause and ask yourself, "Where is the impulse to eat coming from? Am I hungry or emotional? Am I wanting to avoid something, or am I bored?" We think we have free will, but there may be underlying habits that are driving our impulses. Be curious, ask questions, and get to know what drives you.

Imagine all the thoughts that go through your mind every day — how many go unchecked and create stories? Thoughts multiply when left unchecked. When you notice yourself saying things like, "I don't know why I do that. That is just who I am," you allow unconscious programming to run you. Get to know yourself by simply asking yourself, "Why do I do that?" Take some time to enquire about whether your soul is making choices or conditioned responses.

28. PICTURE YOUR GOALS

Clarify your intention for your desires.

There is no need to know the way towards a goal. Enjoy the journey, and open your awareness to synchronistic events you can embrace with action. Dream big.

Message

It's time now to create something new. It may be an experience, a relationship, a job, or a new career. It may be expanding on what you have in your life already. You are a creative soul, yearning to design a life aligned with your highest potential. This all accumulates to create a goal, desire, or endpoint that you believe will improve your life experience.

Your soul's objective is to embrace life through physical existence, aiming for personal growth, expansion, and joyful experiences. Your soul knows what you truly desire, and it will drop hints and ideas you'll feel as inspirations that move you towards setting a desired goal. Goal setting is like delegating to a universal director. Your job is to align with the feeling of your goal's vibrating frequency and allow that to permeate your life, so you find gratitude and joy on the way to it. Recognise how you will feel when your desire arrives and apply it whenever possible. Trust that the universal director has everything under control. When action is required, your director will bring your attention to it, either through a decision that is needed from you or another inspiration. Inspired action means focusing on activities that resonate with, and contribute to, your desired goal.

To strengthen your desired goal, use it in your meditation practice by visualising yourself living your chosen desire or imagining going to a future time where your desire is a part of your life.

Create a vision board in the masterclass to embody the message and work towards your goal by feeling its vibrational frequency.

Conscious Creator Masterclass: Creating a Vision Board

The previous masterclass introduced the concept of free will. This masterclass introduces your ability to use your free will to create a specific pathway for your dreams and desires. The goal becomes a magnet, pulling you towards it through your actions and choices.

Vision Board Exercise

Auspicious times are good for starting a project. If a date is important to you, this timing can help reinforce a desired goal. Some examples of auspicious times are birthdays, New Year, the new moon (see the *Moon Illumination* card), solstices or equinoxes. But the best time to begin creating your new life is NOW. Create a vision board whenever it feels right for you.

This technique primes your mind and body for your desires, serving as a daily meditation tool to bolster your goals. Create multiple boards, ideally up to seven, to visualise different dreams. These boards, whether digital or physical, can include images that inspire gratitude, elevate memories, or represent your bucket list. Select images that evoke excitement or inspiration, or trigger goosebumps. Ask your manifestation name or use the word 'assist' to confirm if the images are a good match. Choose the board colour and arrange the pictures. Remove any images that don't resonate and add more if needed. Let the board sit for 24 hours before affixing the images.

For a physical board, the materials you'll most likely need are:

- An A4, or bigger, piece of cardboard for the background. If making more than one, use different colours that match your topic
- Magazines or printed images from online sources
- Scissors and glue/glue stick or spray adhesive
- A fun attitude and an open mind

For a digital board, you will probably need to:

- Open a document in which you can add images or use a vision boarding app. (There are plenty of free and paid apps for all types of devices)
- Gather images from online sources and place them in a folder called 'Vision Board' in your photo folder or app

- Use editing software to crop images
- Have a fun attitude and an open mind

Keep your vision board or image on your device by your bedside. Review it before bed and upon waking for the first 28 days. Afterwards, place it in a visible location or refer to it as needed. Viewing your board will evoke the desired feelings associated with your goals. Spend a minute feeling these emotions with your eyes closed. On each full moon, review and document manifested desires in your journal. After a year, create a new board for fresh energy and renewed focus.

Journal Work

Create two pages in your journal called 'Vision Board Desire List' and 'Vision Board Manifested List'. Write or draw a list of desired topics in the Vision Board Desire List, including the date and names of your vision board. Add to this list whenever your life inspires a new topic.

During each full moon, record or illustrate successful manifestations in the Vision Board Manifested List. Include the date and the specific board. You made this happen and inspired new topics for future vision boards; you are becoming a deliberate creator. Enjoy your creations!

29. MOON ILLUMINATION

Track your manifestations with lunar cycles.

Desires are coming, even if you can't see them yet. The moon provides an easy way to record how you feel and track manifested evidence to keep your focus and faith, however many cycles it takes.

Message

The moon reflects what you long for each night into your dreams. Over the next few nights, take special note of your dreams. You are being prepared for a dream to come true. When you experience it in your dreams, it feels possible. Your feelings generate emotions and hormones that carry your dream experience into your waking world, where it becomes a future memory pulling you towards it.

Our beautiful moon stirs your emotions and amplifies dreams and desires. Moonlight is the light that reaches Earth from the moon, consisting mainly of sunlight, with some starlight and reflected Earthlight. Its silvery rays shine into your inner world of all possibilities, asking you, "How do you want your life to feel? How will that look?"

Moons reflect the collective and individual consciousness of the planets they orbit. Let the moon's gentle light touch your innermost self, bringing to your awareness anything that requires healing or deserves recognition — whether it's a hidden talent, passion, or life mission. Let it all be illuminated, enlightened by your inner mystery.

Magical moonlight offers a way to track your manifestation mastery through its monthly cycle. Your emotive impulses are constructing pathways of creation that you can measure and record. It is a simple way to reflect on the time it takes to create specific desires. In that time, you can clarify and improve upon your desires. Take joy in the moon's light as you watch your desires unfold in surprising and beautiful ways.

Explore the exercises in the masterclass to embody the message and create a way to map and record your manifestations with the moon's cycle.

Conscious Creator Masterclass: Meeting Your Desires and Inner Creator

The previous masterclass introduced your ability to use your free will and create a specific pathway for your dreams and desires. This masterclass introduces the concept of using the moon's cycle to record and measure the progress of your dreams and desires.

Visualisation
Find a comfortable place to sit or lie down. Place the *Moon Illumination* card at your feet. In your mind, repeat your manifestation name or the word 'lunar' nine times. Gently close your eyes. Sense your body and concentrate on your breathing. Follow your breath inward. Hold for five seconds. Breathe out and release all tension. Relax. Then, focus on the middle of your chest. Sense your breathing moving in and out of your heart.

Imagine the moon gently floating above you. Her moonlight streams towards you as a silvery, shimmering light. You raise your energy to unite with this loving, inspirational, creative light. You move higher and higher, beyond space and time, to visit the mystery, the part of you that lies below, above, and to the sides. Being safely held by silver light allows your body and mind to fill up many reflections of your desires. Float dreamily in this extraordinary place for at least a minute.

When you feel ready to return, tell yourself, "I now tell a new story. I remember who I am, and my desires show up easily." Begin to take deep breaths. Let your breath guide you back to your physical self. Wiggle your toes and fingers. Then, stretch your body and open your eyes.

Reflections and Actions and Journal Work:
Monthly Moon Mapping
The moon radiates different energies during its approximately 28-day cycle. Monthly moon mapping is a simple way to explore and measure your manifestations over four weeks.

Each month, list seven desires. It can take more than a month for desires to manifest, so carry any over to the next month. Each month, you will move closer to your desires or realise they lead you to an even greater desire.

For each month, create four pages, one for each week in your journal, and then follow the instructions under these headings:

Ask — First Week: New Moon Desires
Write or draw seven desires. If you get stuck, consider the different areas of your life, such as spirituality, finance, love, fun, friends, family, creativity, career, health, or wellbeing. When you ask, the desire has a place to grow for you to receive.

Contemplate — Second Week: First Quarter Moon Awareness
Start with the first desire on your new moon list. Focus your awareness on the desire. Ask yourself, "How would I feel if I lived this desire now?" Write or draw anything in your life that has the flavour of your desire. New understandings about a desire are also a manifestation. Repeat with your other six desires. Focused awareness builds momentum and belief.

Receive — Third Week: Full Moon Celebration
List and celebrate anything you have received from your seven new moon desires. If you can't think of any, write or draw any achievements from the past two weeks. Finding ways to celebrate your life keeps you aligned with the vibration of receiving.

Refine — Fourth Week: Last Quarter Moon Integration
Start with the first item on your new moon list of desires. Write or draw anything you learnt or understood from the previous three weeks. Integration creates space for re-evaluation and refinement of next month's list of desires.

30. DIMENSIONS

Diverse perceptions.

Dimensions are different layers of information, filling your life with colour, texture, richness, and immense knowledge. As you learn more, your refined values and desires create a more precise path towards manifestation.

Message

You are about to learn about a past event that will paint a different picture and alter your perception. What you thought was true was your viewpoint at that time. When you learn more, the story will evolve to set yourself or others free of hurt or blame.

There are so many ways to engage with, and interpret, the world. We all have different points of view, like puzzle pieces creating a bigger picture. Imagine for a moment that you have access to all perceptions and information about a story that has been defining you. Your story is just one perception. When you experience and see numerous points of view, the story no longer holds you back, and eventually you will gain wisdom from your story.

Exploring various dimensions entails impartially when considering multiple perspectives and enhancing the depth and vibrancy of your manifestations. Your perspective is valuable and contributes to broader understanding. Embrace diverse viewpoints to expand your knowledge and choices, transforming the unknown into familiar terrain and fostering courage.

Dimensions are layers of perception existing simultaneously in every space and time. While they may seem separate from our three-dimensional perspective, they provide various viewpoints to understand creation. Think of dimensions as distinct ways to measure something from different angles, offering unique perspectives rather than destinations for happiness or enlightenment. Explore the exercises in the masterclass to embody the message and create new perspectives.

Conscious Creator Masterclass: A Journey of Perception

The previous masterclass provided an easy way to record and quantify your manifestations. This masterclass introduces the concept of dimensions to evaluate the variations and different perspectives of creations, desires, and manifestations.

Visualisation

Find a comfortable place to sit. Place the *Dimensions* card at your feet and rest your hands on your lap. Ask the spirit of your manifesting name to be with you so they can observe your sensations and perceptions. Close your eyes softly and tenderly.

Breathe deeply. Focus on the middle of your chest. The energy in your heart centre swirls into a flower-of-life pattern that opens a portal. Breathe naturally as your consciousness travels through your portal into the mind of the universe.

You are gently floating in space, feeling relaxed and calm. Direct your attention to the top of your head, scan your body slowly and release any tension or tightness. Repeat until your body feels soft and relaxed. Breathe deeply and direct your awareness to your mind. Recall a story that you tell often. Imagine the landscape of the story is floating above you like a movie. Introduce all the characters and have them play out the story with you. As the story plays out, enter each character's point of view. You are collecting information, and you are safe. Feel the sensations and emotions. There is no need to come to conclusions; allow yourself to experience these unique perspectives.

Float in space and allow this information to move through you. Whatever feels right for you will join your consciousness. Stay here for at least two minutes.

When you are ready, float back through your flower-of-life portal into your heart, then feel your consciousness moving through your whole body. Ask the spirit of your manifestation name to add its viewpoint. Take three deep, slow breaths. You are now fully back in your reality. Wiggle and stretch your body, then open your eyes.

Journal Work

After the visualisation, write or draw about the different viewpoints of each character in your story. Then, add the viewpoint of the spirit of your manifesting name.

Write or draw any conclusions you come to. Has the story changed? What is the story helping you to learn or heal? Go easy — whatever you felt in the past is not wrong, it was simply your point of view then. Now, you know more and are expanding into spiritual maturity.

Reflections and Actions

Different states of consciousness brought on by meditating, sleeping, alcohol, drugs, or food will give you a different experience of your reality. Next time you are about to eat chocolate, pay attention to how you feel before and after eating it. What difference do you notice?

Next time you are outside, walk around a tree; each angle represents a different dimension. When you stand in front of the tree, that is what you see. You know the tree is more than its front. Walk to the back of the tree. What information is the tree sharing with you that differs from the front view? Keep moving around it to see and collate other points of view. When you have finished, thank the tree for this co-creation. You have both expanded your perceptions.

You will know when you step into a different dimension or point of view. The impressions they leave will vibrate through you like the resonance of a great bell. It may manifest as energy ripples sliding up and down your spine, arms, head, or around your hips. You may feel lightheaded, and your eyesight may blur. These manifestations are fleeting, lasting from a few seconds to a few hours. If they last any longer, seek medical assistance.

31. THE SOURCE

The sound of the universe coming into being.

Your soul is a part of the Source on a journey, and you are part of your soul on a journey. OM echoes a beautiful vibration, reminding you of the connection to the Source and the desire to lovingly create and grow.

Message

You are ready to begin something completely new. You are always young enough to follow a passion. The vibrations of your desires consistently pulsate from you, shining like a lighthouse through a dark night. No matter what happens, this pure devotion and eagerness for life will guide you towards an open sea of infinite potential. This is your soul expressing and enjoying the ride as you explore the variations of what is important to you.

Just like your soul is learning and growing through you, imagine the Source as the soul of the universe experiencing and expanding itself through every stream of consciousness, every thought, dream, and desire. The universe came into existence from an impulse of eagerness and fascination or perhaps from a sense of solitude, seeking companionship. This creation mirrors the birth of your desires. The symbol on the card represents the sound of the universe as it came into being. Chanting OM makes it easier to align with your soul and the soul of the universe — the Source and the energy of pure, boundless possibilities.

Imagine the mind of the universe — the Source, realised. The words "I AM" float into its mind, followed by the statement, "I am, so I can be or do whatever I desire." As it thought itself into being, its first question, "I am, so what, or who, can I become?", charged its core with so much energy that it burst outward in waves of light and sound, represented by the OM symbol on the card. The universe began to breathe and sing. Each breath of light reaches further into eternity to create shapes with consciousness. The Source is where you come from and go to.

Explore the exercises in the masterclass to embody the message and discover your potential.

Conscious Creator Masterclass: Experience Pure Potential

The previous masterclass on dimensions provided an easy way to evaluate the variations and levels of inner and outer desires, and manifestations. This masterclass introduces the concept of a desire in its beginning phase as it evolves from pure potential.

Visualisation
Find a comfortable place to sit. Place *The Source* card at your feet and rest your hands gently on your lap. Close your eyes softly and

tenderly. Focus on the middle of your chest. Slowly take a deep breath, and as you exhale, chant OM. Repeat two more times. Your body will subtly vibrate as you align with the frequency of OM. A portal opens through the centre of the symbol. Breathe naturally as your consciousness travels through the portal into the pure potential of space.

Floating serenely through space, you look down at your hands and notice you are holding a sphere of clear quartz crystal. Gaze into the centre of your sphere as it slowly expands and surrounds you until you are at its centre. You feel a sense of familiarity, like being with the most loving family. You have become a point of light at the centre of potential. Within your sphere, you are floating on an ocean of boundless possibilities. Deep within, a voice emerges, "I AM, I AM. What can I be now, I AM?" An ocean of possibilities swirls. It feels like a spiral moving upwards within you. Then, an explosion of ideas emerges from the top of your head. More and more dreams and desires come from you to fill up your sphere. Stay here, experiencing your pure potential for at least one minute.

When you feel ready, take a deep breath and breathe that potential into your heart. You can connect to your dreams and the "I AM" whenever you want by closing your eyes, touching your heart and chanting "OM" three times. Float back through the OM symbol portal into your heart, then guide your awareness through your body. Take three deep, slow breaths. You are now fully back in your reality. Wiggle and stretch your body, then open your eyes.

Journal Work

Following the visualisation, document your deepest dreams and which one you anticipate arriving next, along with your thoughts on the universe's inception. Recognise these signs as the start of a new chapter in your life.

Reflections and Actions: How to Chant OM

When chanting OM, it is pronounced as the three syllables A-U-M, dissipating into silence.

- The first syllable, A, is pronounced as a prolonged "aaaa" from the back of your throat. Your mouth is open. A vibrating sensation will start in your solar plexus and move up into your chest. This is the shortest syllable.
- The second syllable, U, is pronounced as a prolonged "ooo", gradually progressing forwards along your upper palate. Your lips form an O shape, and your throat will subtly vibrate. This syllable is chanted slightly longer than the first.
- The third syllable, M, is a prolonged "mmmm". Your mouth is closed, and your front teeth gently touch. Your whole mouth and face will gently vibrate. This syllable is extended the most.
- The last part is about three seconds of silence before taking another deep breath to begin the next OM.

Think of A as creation, U as manifestation, M as freedom, and silence as appreciation. Chanting OM seven times has the following effects:

- Relaxes the body, regulates the nervous system, and calms the mind

- Increases your energy levels and endorphins, and helps you feel refreshed
- Activates mindfulness and heartfulness
- Brings dreams and desires to the forefront of your mind
- Brings clarity on a specific desire

Close your eyes. Slowly take a deep breath, and as you exhale, chant OM.

32. DUALITY

Contrasts of desires.

When both sides are explored and appreciated, you move into the centre. Accept the friction of duality needed for desires to manifest. How would you know joy if not for sadness?

Message

Today is a day to see all things as they are, without opinion or resistance. There is no need to choose one over another. This is easier said than done, as we have been taught to label and categorise everything to feel secure. Drop your subjective bias and see things as a whole, then move back into your heart centre and create from a balanced perspective.

Choices are clear and decisions easily made when our internal and external realities are integrated. This leads to feelings of certainty as there is no resistance to your fulfilment. From this integrated space, when you can scan the myriad possibilities in the manifested world, you will feel surer of your desires and not feel overwhelmed. You become grateful for your decisions now, and all the ones you will make in the future. You begin to effortlessly flow with life.

The symbol on the image is called the *vesica piscis*, and is the basis of the 'flower of life' diagram. No matter how often it splits and moves outward, there is always a link back to itself within the intersection of circles. It floats under a lemniscate, or eternity symbol, as all circles are a part of the eternal and not judged, just experienced.

From a one-dimensional perspective, observation occurs without interaction. The first dimension holds the idea, while the second shapes the atmosphere, fostering desires through contrasting viewpoints. 'Purpose' (positive charge) radiates and creates, while 'mission' (negative charge) absorbs and envisions a continuous dance of creation. Each aspect complements the other, both stemming from Source energy and integral to measuring life in the third dimension. The Purpose pushes you out of alignment to experience something different so the mission can return you to alignment to reflect, calibrate, and integrate experiences to your authenticity.

Explore the exercises in the masterclass to embody the message and balance your viewpoint.

Conscious Creator Masterclass: Looking at Your Mirror Image

The previous masterclass presented the beginning of desire as it evolves from pure potential. This masterclass introduces the concept of duality as a way to measure and clarify your desires, purpose, and mission.

Visualisation

Find a comfortable place to sit. Place the *Duality* card at your feet and rest your hands gently on your lap. In your mind, repeat your manifestation name or the word 'contrast' nine times. Close your eyes softly and tenderly. Breathe deeply. Focus on the middle of your chest. The energy in your heart centre begins to swirl into an eternity symbol that opens a portal. Breathe naturally as your consciousness travels through your portal into the universe.

Floating serenely through a blue and purple space, you arrive at the centre of two overlapping spheres. A magical mirror appears. You stand before it and see yourself reflected as the beautiful light being you are. Your soul shines its eternity into your heart, and you begin to realise you are much more than you believe. It begins to show the light and shadow parts of you. You are everything you love and don't love. The contrast between positive and negative creates more straightforward and significant questions. What will you choose?

Your magical mirror is reflecting your soul self, glowing and vibrating. So much love pours from your reflection; you have never felt so loved. Lift your hands to touch their reflection. As you connect and merge with your soul self, you glow and vibrate like your reflection, the mirror dissolves, and you embrace. You have become your reflection. Now pull to you people and circumstances that vibrate in fullness. You don't need anything from each other. Instead, you will encourage each other to be everything you can be. This is freedom. Stay here for at least two minutes to integrate your soul beauty and path.

When you feel ready, take a deep breath. Float back through the blue and purple into the portal. Breathe deeply, knowing that each day, you are rebirthed through the cosmic womb that is the overlapping circles. From now on, intend to enter each day in truth, in the overlap where the wisdom of the moment is. Then shift towards one of the realities, depending on your thoughts and experiences, and where you want your life to go.

Your consciousness flows through the eternity symbol into your body. Take three deep, slow breaths. You are now fully back in your reality. Wiggle and stretch your body, then open your eyes.

Journal Work
After the visualisation, write or draw about what you saw and felt when you experienced your reflection in the mirror. What has it inspired you to create more of in your life? For example, it could be changes to how you think, eat, work, or communicate.

Reflections and Actions
Dualistic thinking is the perception that one way of looking at something is right, while the opposing perspective is wrong. Even though we live in a dualistic realm, thinking through a frame of 'one or another' will give you a lopsided perspective. The idea is to collate as much information as possible to make an informed decision.

The next time you are debating with another, ask yourself, "What would my life be like if I thought the opposite? What could I learn about myself?" You may like to record any findings in your journal.

For a few hours a day, turn off the television, put down your phone, and tune in to your inner glow of creativity and entertainment. This will grow confidence in listening to your inner knowing, instead of being swayed by others' opinions.

You will drive yourself mad if you try to hold both sides of something in your mind. Learning to let everything just be as it is can be difficult for adults — we have spent a long time collating information and then sorting it into piles. The next time you observe something, imagine it is the first time you are looking at it, as if you were a child. Look at it innocently. You are not being naïve, as your past knowledge about this subject is still available to you. Just try it and record your findings.

If you want a bit more of a mind-bending challenge, you can explore the concept of 'non-dualism'. This is the perspective that everything is interconnected, part of a single, unified whole without separate, independent existences, and the world is an illusion created by the mind and the senses.

33. REALITY

Experience your desires.

All your desires exist in the quantum field. Life on Earth allows you to manifest and play with them in the physical reality of time and space for the sheer joy of seeing what you can create.

Message

Here is a vibrant message from the universe: Right here, right now, BE YOU!

When you act on your passion, help will come. You are unique, and no one has ever seen the world how you do. You are a piece of a beautiful puzzle. It's essential to embrace the unique shape that you are because that's the shape that will fit with all the other shapes, who are each being their own individual shapes. If you try to be another shape, you won't fit in, and the big picture of your life will remain elusive. You are not meant to be like everyone else. What you love in another is something you are yet to love in yourself. It lives in you; otherwise, you would not recognise it. Use the lives of others to inspire your passions instead of trying to live them.

Awaken to a new reality through presence, seizing each moment for wisdom to guide your path. Embrace confidence in your journey, as you recognise that where you are is where you need to be. Most of us rush forwards, not taking the time to garner the wisdom that travels with us. Expand your perspective to include the periphery; the answers we seek often lie overlooked in pursuit of our goals.

You are the living expression of the Source. Feel it flow through you, inspiring and illuminating the love in you and all. Broaden your mind beyond the mountains of mass agreements that form the third-dimensional reality, and shake loose any limitations holding you away from your soul dreams. You are a light pioneer, exploring new territory for the joy of experiencing life. You will transcend this trinity by grounding into, and falling in love with, the wonderment and perfection of the third dimension.

Explore the exercises in the masterclass to embody the message and live passionately.

Conscious Creator Masterclass: Waking Up from Reality

The previous masterclass covered the concept of duality to measure and clarify desire, and your life path. This masterclass reminds you that the only way to manifest your desires fully is to be grounded, appreciating your life in third-dimensional reality.

Visualisation

Find a comfortable place to sit. Place the *Reality* card at your feet. Rest your hands gently on your lap. In your mind, repeat your manifestation name or the word 'life' nine times. Close your eyes softly and tenderly. Breathe deeply. Focus on the middle of your chest. The energy in your heart centre begins to swirl into many layers of your heart. There is a portal at the centre. Breathe naturally as your consciousness travels through your portal into the universe.

Floating serenely through hues of blues and reds, you experience the many layers of your heart as your passions and desires to create in this lifetime. Anchor the universal light through your heart and hear the soulful tones of your divine plane, your reason for being here in this life. This is your essence. Feel the light from your heart burst forth, illuminating everything around you, thoroughly bathing you in the light of your heart. You are beautiful and perfect, right here, right now. Be here in this space, at this moment, and allow yourself to see the beauty within and all around you.

This reality has infinite paths of creation. What will you create? New realisations and ways to live your life begin to float around you. Stay here for at least three minutes to bring more dreams into being.

When you feel ready, take a deep breath. Float back peacefully through the hues of blues and reds into the portal. Your consciousness flows through your heart into your whole body. Take three deep, slow breaths. You are now fully back in your reality. Wiggle and stretch your body, then open your eyes.

Journal Work

After the visualisation, write or draw about three new ways to live your life, free and improved. You can't change anything by fighting what has already been created. Create a new way that supersedes the old way to bring about change. Let your imagination play. You don't have to know the details, they will come later. If you already love your life, consider how you can make it even better. If you want to change your life but feel apprehensive, try changing your perspective or approach.

Reflections and Actions
Awakening

When you awaken to your truth, the feeling is so incredible and freeing that you may feel it is your responsibility to help everyone feel this good. Awakening others is not your role — your role is to feel the best you can in every moment and be balanced within yourself. Allow your soul, your higher self, the Source, and the universe to shine through you and inspire others to choose to see the world differently, if they so desire. Whatever they decide to do is up to them. You have the choice to love you and all. Everyone is at different levels of perception and consciousness. Wherever anyone is, is perfect for them in their life at that moment. No one must change for you to feel love for them because you are love.

Say these questions and answers to yourself to assist in awakening into each moment, to really enjoy and create fully:

- Where am I? — I am here.
- What time is it? — The time is now.
- What am I? — I am this moment.

Awakening is the dissolving of anything that does not align with your soul.

Space and Time Definition

- Desires manifest in space into a physical form with height, depth, and width. This is more exciting than being a concept in your mind. Now, you can play with it, measure it, and create more variations of your desires.
- Desires manifest in time — into the past, present, and future. Time is the space between your manifestations, so you experience them one at a time to fine-tune, clarify, and build on past experiences.

A fun way to practise presence and mindfulness is to complete a jigsaw puzzle. To develop a more profound feeling of presence and a deeper understanding of how things fit together, do a physical jigsaw puzzle, not an online or app jigsaw. When you move the pieces into their place, your bodily knowing, certainty, and courage expand and encourage you to go out to create your desires.

34. BEYOND SPACETIME

Measure accomplishments and build on them.

As you spend more time on this planet, you gather aspects of your multidimensional self for healing and renewal. This includes past memories, future projections, and the unfolding present moment. Behold the opening access to the fluid nature of time through multiple timelines and experiences.

Message

Your relationship with time is changing. This is an indicator that your awareness and consciousness are expanding. You might be experiencing time flying by, wondering why time seems to disappear. Don't worry, your life isn't disappearing — you are simply focused elsewhere.

Sometimes you feel so overwhelmed and busy, as if you have lived a whole day in your mind before it even starts. Your mind is in the future, and your body is a little confused about where it is. In this state, living in the present can seem tedious: you long for the end of the day so that you can relax. But you sit down and can't relax, it seems like a waste of time. The solace and connection you seek is with your soul, which exists in the present moment. You need time to reflect, to feel what is right for you. When you are so busy filling space in your day, there is no time to decide whether this thing you are experiencing is right for you. You have a choice: go about your day as you always have and produce the same results, or pause, and balance and line up with your desires.

Time serves as a measure of manifestations, enhancing our appreciation of the physical experience. Embrace your entirety beyond perceived density. You are light interwoven into creation, traversing planes with freedom beyond time's constraints. Pause in any moment, breathe, and exist fully in the present. Time becomes fluid, pulsating, expanding, and collapsing simultaneously, offering boundless opportunities for innovation and love. Embrace this moment to manifest love, allowing time to unveil its myriad manifestations.

Time is changing for everyone. As we grow and evolve, our perceptions shift. It will be a different experience for each individual, depending on their level of consciousness. The structures of our world, where everything had its place and time, are becoming more fluid. This is the natural evolution of life. Things we were told were certain and structured are less rigid, ushering us into new ways to co-create in the world.

Explore the exercises in the masterclass to embody the message and discover the expansiveness of time.

Conscious Creator Masterclass: Actualising Different Possibilities

The previous masterclass reminded you that the only way to fully manifest your desires is to be grounded in third-dimensional reality. This masterclass introduces a different concept of time.

When you dream, you are in a fourth-dimensional perspective. This preps your mind to accept that you can manifest your dreams and desires. As well as through your dreams, you can access the fourth dimension through meditation or a shift in consciousness, sometimes called an out-of-body experience.

Visualisation

Find a comfortable place to sit. Place the *Beyond Spacetime* card at your feet and rest your hands gently on your lap. In your mind, repeat your manifestation name or the word 'fantasy' nine times. Close your eyes softly and tenderly. Breathe deeply. Focus on the middle of your chest. The energy in your heart centre swirls into a portal. Breathe naturally as your consciousness travels through your portal into the universe.

Floating dreamily through a mist of red and rainbows, you notice a network of crisscrossing lines that intersect with points of light below you. The points of light are your life experiences, while the lines are timelines. Look a little closer, and you will see multiple timelines flowing through your experiences, producing endless wonder.

Bring to your mind an experience you want to see from a different point of view. Peruse the network of manifestations and timelines below you. Your focused intention is lighting up one experience in a brighter way, making it easy to locate. Imagine you touch that point, and suddenly, it is playing out on a huge movie screen. Just like a dream, you can see how an event plays out. You can go anywhere or do anything. You may be in another body or at another time. Your dream movies are preparing you to believe in the manifestation of your dreams. If you can dream it, you will believe and create it. Explore, you are safe. Play in this space for at least four minutes.

When you feel ready, take a deep breath. Float back peacefully through the mist of red and rainbow into the portal. Your consciousness flows through your heart and into your whole body. Take three deep, slow breaths. You are now fully back in your reality. Wiggle and stretch your body, then open your eyes.

Journal Work

After the visualisation, write or draw about your observations and experiences of an alternative way to create and live a desire. There are many paths to your desires. Open your mind and heart to different approaches, and never let go of your dreams.

Reflections and Actions

Receive any information gently by allowing it to join your mind and expand your consciousness slowly. If it makes little sense, let it be a part of your mind reference, like buying a book you haven't read yet.

Read books or watch TV series or movies that explore different or alternate timelines and time travel:

- *The Man in the High Castle* by Philip K. Dick
- *Solaris* by Stanisław Lem (1961)
- *11/22/63* by Stephen King (2011)
- *The Time Machine* by H.G. Wells (1895)
- *The Matrix* series of movies (1999–2021)
- *Contact* (1997)
- *Inception* (2010)
- *The Time Traveler's Wife* (2009)
- *Midnight in Paris* (2011)
- *Everything Everywhere All at Once* (2022)
- *2001: A Space Odyssey* (1968)

Research the Mandela effect, a phenomenon where people collectively misremember events, historical facts, and other famous pop culture moments. It was named by paranormal researcher Fiona Broome, who thought the late South African president, Nelson Mandela, had died in the 1980s. His actual death was in 2013.

We are at a point in our collective consciousness where we are grasping the idea of a holographic universe, parallel universes, and quantum timelines. Because of our expanding consciousnesses, this reality is becoming more fluid, causing slippages into parallel and other realities. I believe the events themselves have not been deliberately changed. Instead, a slight change or adjustment happened in the timeline leading up to the event. Maybe it is to remind us, in a fun-loving way, that we can change anything. It is a peculiar phenomenon, and when you check it out, you may think you are going a little crazy.

35. AN ELEVATED PERSPECTIVE

An ascended master's point of view.

Ascended masters are self-realised light beings, from a different dimension of perception. They communicate through your soul and intuition, collapsing all contrasts into the present moment so you can be free of any bias and see the entire picture.

Message

Glorious fifth-dimensional ascended masters accompany your soul as it journeys through the experience of your body and life. You have expanded to a frequency that enables you to meet them in your inner world. They are excitedly preparing you to remember and embrace your unique offering in this life, while observing your life from a higher perspective to see the most auspicious path for you and assisting you to achieve your dreams and desires. These enlightened beings understand the patterns and connections between all things and how to channel your soul's purpose to your heart. Embrace their perspective to gain insight into life's meaning. You hold the power to decide your actions, knowing they will always guide you.

The fifth dimension is a brighter, lighter version of the third dimension, simultaneously existing at a higher frequency. Tuning into this vibration and making it your predominate frequency allows you to manifest your desires quicker.

Ascended masters are light beings who become self-realised and have raised their vibration to feel their full stream of consciousness at will, always with love. They can quickly move through the dimensions.

Self-realisation is the awareness of our complete and inseparable union with the Divine. This also means that the ego-self knows itself so clearly, lovingly, and wisely that it is no longer run by the shadow. When one is in the illuminated state or self-realised, there ceases to be any more inner or outer drama. The personal ego-self has surrendered fully and willingly into the loving embrace of the soul.

Ascended masters are activating your higher will. How willing are you to live your life from this higher perspective? Allow your expanded consciousness to treat you, and the world, with love and compassion. We all have backstories that bring us into this moment and underpin our behaviour. This is not to excuse behaviours, but a way to help humanity become better.

Explore the exercises in the masterclass to embody the message and become open to understanding the purpose and reason for your life.

Conscious Creator Masterclass: You Are an Ascended Master

The previous masterclass provided a new relationship with time. This masterclass introduces a higher perception that brings purpose and reason to your life.

Visualisation

Find a comfortable place to sit. Place the *An Elevated Perspective* card at your feet and rest your hands gently on your lap. In your mind, repeat your manifestation name or the word 'wise' nine times. Close your eyes, breathe deeply, and focus on the middle of your chest. The energy in your heart centre swirls into a portal. Breathe naturally as your consciousness travels through your portal into the universe.

Floating peacefully upon the geometric fabric of time and space, you move through blue and purple nebulous clouds into a golden ray of light. Immediately, you are transported upwards. You feel a sense of ease and freedom pour through you. Floating on this golden ray of light, you are amazed to see many other light beings around you. They gather around, interested in you. They are ascended masters, and some are part of your soul family. During this time, while you meditate, you are one of them. This part of you always exists in the fifth dimension, shining your soul's truth upon you always.

The ascended masters ask you to look down upon your life, spread out in a circle below you. As you gaze down, the reasons for everything in your life arises in your mind. You understand the absolute perfection in everything you have experienced. There is no right nor wrong; there is just the experience. Your soul and the entire universe have grown from your experiences. The masters around you beam a sense of gratitude towards you. You were never judged; you were simply loved for courageously exploring the third dimension.

From this higher understanding of your life, spend five minutes sending love and gratitude to your physical body and life.

When you feel ready, take a deep breath. Float downwards on your golden ray and through the nebulous clouds of blue and purple into the portal. Your consciousness flows through your heart into your body. Take three deep, slow breaths. You are now fully back in your reality. Wiggle and stretch your body, then open your eyes.

Journal Work

After the visualisation, write or draw the revelations you had about your life. Looking at an event from a different perspective will give you more information to work with. Sometimes, what we thought was true was a conclusion from when we experienced it. Changing a story or narrative can be an emotional, revealing process. Go easy; you are becoming more of yourself, growing, and expanding your awareness.

Write or draw about any experiences you may have had with an ascended master, angel, or light being. Were they helping you see a different perspective?

Reflections and Actions

Clear your mind of yesterday's grime to enable a clear connection to your light beings. Meditation is as necessary as a daily shower.

Five minutes daily will quiet your mind, calm your body, and allow an unshakable peace to move through you. You can even do this when you shower. Imagine the water flowing from the shower head becomes a liquid light that washes away any worries, upsets, or negative energy.

Research and listen to brainwave entrainment or binaural beats meditation music. Add it to your regular meditation practice to help expand your inner world and soul connection.

Before sleeping, place a small amethyst crystal on your forehead for two minutes and ask for an ascended master or insight to come through your dreams. Then, place the crystal near your bed.

36. SPIRITUAL ALCHEMY

A framework that supports manifestations.

Spiritual alchemy is the art of change, transformation, and inner liberation. The higher mind of your soul is a spiritual alchemist who can seemingly create anything out of thin air. This information will unfold and reveal itself throughout your spiritual journey.

Message

Your ability to be a master manifestor lies within. To reveal this expert part of yourself, you go through spiritual alchemy. Imagine your life is like a computer game — your journey has been composed of different adventures to explore and pieces of wisdom to collect. As you do this, you level up and transform your experience of reality.

From a third-dimensional perspective, you use a range of emotions to represent wants and needs to create your desires. Emotions are the fuel that creates this reality and allows us to be empathic and accountable about what we manifest.

But in the sixth dimension, as the master manifestor, you have no physical body to create emotions. As a light being, you are always in a balanced state. Everything created and experienced is vibrational. Here desires happen quickly, which could seem exciting, but imagine your life if everything you thought about turned up immediately?

Because sixth-dimensional beings can create at will and don't need an emotional body, they need our point of view to bring accountability and meaning to their creations. We are co-creating with them. They share how to manifest beyond emotion, and we share the feelings that bring meaning and accountability to the creative process. We are all in this together.

When you ask, your desire automatically reverberates through the dimensions as a unique frequency manifesting in the non-physical realm. In the sixth dimension, you, as the master manifestor, catch this frequency and instantly weave light and dark waves into infinite options for your third-dimensional self to experience. Your job in the third dimension is to get ready to receive by matching the vibrational pattern.

Spiritual alchemy transforms all your lead into gold, meaning you allow, heal, and let go of anything resisting your desires. Then, you can deliberately shift your emotions into balance and a state of allowing, also called love. In this space, you vibrate at the level of your master manifestor and feel your way into the frequency of your desire. You become a match and attract into your earthly reality many different variations of your desire for you to play with. The longer you stay in this vibration, the more variations you manifest.

Explore the exercises in the masterclass to embody the message and connect with your master manifestor.

Conscious Creator Masterclass: Become an Instant Manifestor

The previous masterclass provided a higher perception to bring a wise purpose and reason to your life. This masterclass introduces your master manifestor and vibrational creation process.

Visualisation

In the image, the light being sits on a lotus, beaming waves of light through a *sri yantra* above their head. *Yantras* are used as points of focus during meditation and reflection. 'Sri' loosely means 'respect, grace, or light'. The *sri yantra* is a geometric representation of OM — the sound of creation. It contains nine interlocking triangles to bring balance to the heart and mind. The lotus flower is a remarkable water lily that grows in mud. No matter what you have experienced, you will always blossom.

Find a comfortable place to sit. Place the *Spiritual Alchemy* card at your feet and rest your hands gently on your lap. In your mind, repeat your manifestation name or the word 'design' nine times. Close your eyes softly and tenderly. Breathe deeply. Focus on the middle of your chest. The energy in your heart centre begins to swirl into a portal. Breathe naturally as your consciousness travels through your portal into the universe.

You float through space on the other side of the portal, becoming the being on the card's image. Gently sit upon your lotus. It communicates with you that you are worthy of all that you desire. Above you a *sri yantra* shines, a reminder of the balanced, unconditional you. Imagine you can create anything. Whatever you think of — whoosh! An instant manifestation floats before you. When you bring something else to mind, the preceding one fades from view and your new thought manifests. You no longer create as you do in the third dimension, through your emotional wants and needs. Instead, you create through vibration and frequency, which reverberates through every dimension. There is no space or time, so you will experience it instantly as a hologram that fills your being with the experience of it. You are no longer creating to survive, but to thrive.

Enjoy several minutes of being your master manifestor. Create. Create. And create ...

When you feel ready, take a deep breath. Your consciousness flows through your heart and into your body. Take three deep, slow breaths. You are now fully back in your reality. Wiggle and stretch your body, then open your eyes.

Journal Work
After the visualisation, write or draw about your instant manifestations. Do they seem more possible now? Do you believe you are ready for them?

Reflections and Actions
Spiritual Alchemy transforms your lead into gold — in essence, you learn how to convert the neglected, rejected, or painful parts of your life into pathways for personal and collective improvement. When you become your gold, it will be easier to create more extraordinary, empowered desires that inspire anyone around you to create their own gold. Ask your soul for help to do this or seek a healer or therapist to help you. Alchemy is an ancient chemical science and speculative philosophy. Early alchemists

aimed to understand the nature of things, how they were made, and how to make more of them. These questions created a system of chemical procedures, symbology, art, and writings centred around discovering the philosopher's stone, a substance that would transmute base metals into gold, cure any disease, and be the key to eternal life. If this resonates, you can research and even study alchemy.

Consider these ideas of transformation:

- A situation forces you to change.
- Are your beliefs still valid? Question them.
- Let go of outdated beliefs to see through new eyes.
- Through full acceptance, your heart opens to higher vibrations.
- As you experience rebirth, any outdated beliefs will rise to be released.
- Contrast still exists. It is how to create bigger.
- Your inner gold shines and becomes an inspiration for new desires.

37. ILLUMINATION

An angelic view of pure information.

The angelic seventh dimension is a clear, inner space that has merged universal data into pure streams of knowing, shining into every cell of your body. You will experience this as a light bulb moment that helps create your desires.

Message

You are activating the star that you are. Your inner sun shines brighter to illuminate your world with more profound wisdom, which expands your consciousness. New questions will drop into your being over the following days as you realise the quality of your life is influenced by the quality of questions you ask.

If you genuinely believe you shape your own reality, you will filter out thoughts from your inner dialogue that don't align with your desires. This does not mean running away or trying to change negative thoughts. Instead, you allow all things—good and bad—to be illuminated so you can consciously choose what inner atmosphere you want. Awakening is a series of illuminations and softenings that turn pain into purpose.

Your purpose is unfolding through your life. It will soon become clearer. If you are unsure, ask your soul or manifestation name for clarity. Ask from your heart, not your intellect. The intellect seeks guidance from external sources, uncertain of its own knowledge, while the heart, confident in its wisdom, seeks internal guidance. The intellect's desire for immediate answers can cause undue stress on the body and mind, whereas the heart allows insights to unfold naturally, in their own time and rhythm. Say out loud, "I am open and allow myself to receive answers." Over the following days and weeks, you will be guided to whatever you need. A book may fall off a shelf, an audiobook or podcast may catch your attention, you may overhear a conversation that gives you a message, or it may come to you in a dream or meditation.

Earth is a beautiful planet to mix up all different perspectives and opinions. Illumination encourages you to really know yourself and understand how your mind and body work, physically and energetically. Spend more time with yourself to polish and shine your inner world. You have spent enough time trying to harmonise with others. It is time to harmonise with yourself and allow your illumination to act as a mirror for others.

Explore the exercises in the masterclass to embody the message and connect with your inner star.

Conscious Creator Masterclass: Experiencing Your Purpose

The previous masterclass provided information to connect to your master manifestor and vibrational creation process. This masterclass introduces ways to enlighten your inner world to learn more about your purpose and motivations.

Visualisation

Find a comfortable place to sit. Place the *Illumination* card at your feet and gently rest your hands on your lap. In your mind, repeat your manifestation name or the word 'light' nine times. Close your eyes softly and tenderly. Breathe deeply. Become aware of your body in the space where you are. Focus on the middle of your chest. A tiny point of light forms and becomes a star.

The star within your heart awakens and swirls in rainbow colours that pulse outward. The light grows larger and larger, and the colours merge into a white light that forms a bubble of light. Feeling loved and embraced, you float within this bubble in your heart space.

As you float through the misty rainbow, you catch sight of an angel observing you. It flashes a smile and gives you a cheeky wink as it glides past you. Something tells you that the angel is an echo of you. It is you, as you are, in this dimension. You call your angel to you. Floating in front of each other, a lightness of heart pours through you. Every part of your body vibrates. Your angel takes you by the hands, and your vibrations lift to meet its frequency. You are each other, communicating without saying words.

Take this opportunity to ask yourself some questions. Allow thoughts, sensations, colours, or feelings to come to you spontaneously.

- What is my purpose? Stay here for one minute and quietly listen.
- How do I bring my purpose into my life? Stay here for one minute and quietly listen.
- Are my dreams and desires related to purpose? Stay here for one minute and quietly listen.
- Where is my purpose right now? Stay here for one minute and quietly listen.

Your angel has some questions for you to ponder and answer in the journal work.

- What did you dream of doing with your life as a child?
- What do you do that doesn't require motivation?
- What do your friends, family, and colleagues say you do well?
- What do you think you do well that gives you joy?
- What are your hobbies?

Reflect on these questions for at least a minute.

Your angel is still holding your hands and wants to play. You spin around each other, as you did as a child. The quicker you spin, the more you see the elements that make up this dimension. You might see waves of colours, numbers, chakra symbols, sacred geometry, the principles of the universe, divinatory practices, or spiritual methods. Each time you come back, something new will illuminate your truth. The spinning slows down, and your angel hugs you and floats from view. Telepathically, they tell you they will always be with you.

When you feel ready, take a deep breath. Float through the misty rainbow through your star and into your heart. Your consciousness flows through your heart and into your body. Take three deep, slow breaths. You are now fully back in your reality. Wiggle and stretch your body, then open your eyes.

Journal Work
Write or draw any answers to the questions that came up during the visualisation (see above).

Reflections and Actions
There are many methods to illuminate your truth and below are some of my favourites. These approaches can help you understand your purpose, psyche, and motivations. I invite you to explore one or more of these. Consider having a personalised chart drawn up and delve into the results, as your choices can provide insight into your self-understanding. Once you've fully explored the process, integrate and transcend the technique.

- Astrology — Western, Chinese, or Vedic
- Numerology
- The Enneagram
- Gene Keys
- Human Design
- Myers–Briggs personality test

38. AKASHA

A quantum field of possibilities.

Within Akasha, originating in the eighth dimension, are the akashic records — a universal network of data permeating all dimensions. Think of it as a library where you can discover your soul's many journeys and desires fulfilled.

Message

You are about to discover fresh information that will enhance how you create your life. It will resonate through you like a beautiful resounding bell, stirring emotions and remembrances of all things you loved and who loved you. Like a dream come to life, you recognise the energy of an interaction that you had in another existence, such as with a tree, animal, place, or person. The container or the agenda may differ, but the essence is the same, which you recognise. This is sometimes called soulmates or soul family. Allow the information to flow; you don't have to understand it all now. However, this information will open a path of allowance, enabling you to effortlessly manifest desires that fully align with your soul's journey.

Your soul is like a drop of water in the cosmic ocean of light called 'Akasha' — a Sanskrit word translating to 'aether, spirit, or sky'. Akasha is all around you, a framework shaped like a torus (a geometric figure resembling a doughnut), a network like the internet. It streams the akashic records—a public library of everything and everyone that has ever been, is, and will be—through all dimensions. As light flows through you, it reflects all your stories and journeys. You can learn about your soul's various stories, which will bring clarity to something you are currently going through.

This information is not only for one person because we are all reflections of the Source. If you are tuned to the network, it will download through you. You can access whatever you need to help understand a problem, expand on a solution, or inspire a new path. You don't have to emotionally attach to any of it, as you always have access to it. Think of this place as a library of stories that give purpose, hope, and meaning to your life's journey and offer infinite possibilities for you to create and manifest.

Explore the exercises in the masterclass to embody the message and receive messages from the akashic records.

Conscious Creator Masterclass: Visit Your Akashic Records

The previous masterclass provided ways to enlighten your inner world to learn more about your purpose and motivations. This masterclass introduces the akashic records, which contain information about your soul's journey, enabling you to clarify your purpose and desires in this life.

Choose a question or topic you want to know more about before beginning this visualisation.

Visualisation

Find a comfortable place to sit. Place the *Akasha* card at your feet and rest your hands gently on your lap. In your mind, repeat your manifestation name or the word 'essence' nine times. Close your eyes softly and tenderly. Breathe deeply. Focus on the middle of your chest. The energy in your heart centre begins to swirl into the shape of the infinity symbol, opening a portal. Breathe naturally as your consciousness travels through your portal into the universe.

Imagine you are floating serenely through misty blue and purple into the centre of this space. Your soul shines its eternalness outward in all directions, and you observe bands of light radiating outwards. It is a network of consciousness connecting all that has ever been, all that is, and all that will be: the akashic records. A particular part of the Akasha lights up. This light is the record of your experiences. You may have been light, a colour, an animal, lived on another planet, or lived on Earth many times. The journey of your soul is unique to you.

Allow your body to be drawn in the direction of the light. You may experience this any way you wish. Today, we will enter the akashic records as if they are a library. Take a breath and reorient yourself back to your heart. Allow your body to direct you to a book. Look at the title. Open the book and thumb through the pages until one catches your heart. Read what is there. You can read another page or return that book and choose another one. Explore your records for several minutes.

Make sure you put all the books back when you have finished. The records must stay here. We are all connected, and for all experiences to make sense, we need all the available information from all points of view.

When you feel ready, take a deep breath. Float through your portal into your eternity symbol and then your heart. Your consciousness flows through your heart into your body. Take three deep, slow breaths. You are now fully back in your reality. Wiggle and stretch your body, then open your eyes.

Journal Work
After the visualisation, write or draw about the information you received from your book/s. Then, write or draw about how the information can help clarify a desire you want to manifest.

Reflections and Actions
Next time you go to a library or bookshop, choose a random book and open it to a random page. What you read will be a message from your soul. Given the unique flow of time in higher dimensions, this message may pertain to your present and future, or offer insight into your past experiences. As information flows through dimensions, its appearance and vibration vary. Geometry serves as the universal language, though currently understood by a select few, including artists, scientists, and spiritually evolved individuals. Consider delving into sacred geometry, starting with the flower of life and platonic solids.

39. BEYOND

Integrate your desire's journey.

Your desire is ready to manifest in ways you have not thought about. Free your desire to be the driving force and organising principle of the next steps to take, and springboard yourself into the next chapter of desire creation.

Message

You are in the middle of a transformation. A new chapter will soon begin. A door is opening to more fantastic dreams and desires. You have outgrown what you thought you couldn't live without. You are about to fall in love with something you didn't even know you wanted. But your soul knows, and it is propelling you forwards. Go easy on yourself. Be the courageous, loving being that you are. You are here to enjoy the journey and can't get it wrong.

Because you can't know an outcome until you live and experience something, all that matters is what you decide to do from this moment on. Obstacles that once seemed impassable now seem insignificant. Those past experiences have empowered you to evolve, grow, and learn to avoid repeating unfavourable situations. Repeating them triggers a cyclical experience, similar yet different and more intense, to alert you to the need to adjust the trajectory of the pattern. Just remember to be kind to yourself and vow to do better.

Your life is yours to live in whatever way is meaningful to you. As you move forwards, you will understand your motives. Experience allows you to handle difficulties better. With each generation, something new grows from the foundations of the one before. You constantly evolve. In the flow of a new chapter, it is exciting to experience what will come.

The Source thought us all into being with the statement, "I AM". From a ninth-dimensional perspective, it realised, "I AM everything, and I AM nothing." The first and ninth dimensions converge. Innocence and wisdom come together in the same space. You are you, and yet you are also the Source. Like you, the universe is a living entity, evolving to experience life in new ways. It is growing with you, creating a new chapter just as you are.

Explore the exercises in the masterclass to embody the message and understand why letting go creates bigger, better desires.

Conscious Creator Masterclass: You Exist Beyond Boundaries

The previous masterclass explained the akashic records containing information about your soul's journey, enabling you to clarify your purpose and desires in this life. This masterclass introduces the cyclical nature of creation — letting go to create more.

Visualisation

Find a comfortable place to sit. Place the *Beyond* card at your feet and rest your hands gently on your lap. In your mind, repeat your manifestation name or the word 'beyond' nine times. Close your eyes. Breathe deeply and allow any thoughts to arise. Let them be with you as you focus on the middle of your chest. The energy in your heart centre begins to swirl into a portal. Breathe naturally as your consciousness travels through your portal into the universe.

You are floating through misty blue and purple into the centre of this space. You begin to see your thoughts floating around you. A doorway comes into focus in the space between the words of your thoughts. Walk through any doorway into a world of wisdom beyond thinking. You are now floating in a fantastic space created by your thoughts. It is like discovering a massive, magical room in your house that you didn't know existed. Explore and play, you will not lose yourself. You will always know who you are, and you are becoming more of who you are. Feel yourself vibrating, expanding, and growing.

You are experiencing all dimensions at the same time. In every one, you are having different experiences. You are infinite, eternal, every-thing and no-thing. You are creating the journey of your life, so keep going. An expanse opens above, allowing you to float upwards into the creative heart of the universe. A loving energy surrounds you, encouraging you to keep experiencing, experimenting, integrating, and transcending your yesterdays to create bigger and better desires to play with in the future.

Place your hands on your heart and feel the creative heart of the universe pulsing with the rhythm of your heart. You are one with all. Float in this space of pure light and love. You watch as a tiny point of light begins to pulse, creating waves of different colours. You tune in to the vibration of the waves and hear, "I AM, so what, or who, can I become?" You are watching a new thought or even a new universe being created. Ride the waves of newness for at least a minute.

When you feel ready, take a deep breath and float downwards through the creative heart of the universe, back through the doorway between your thoughts, and into the misty blue and purple. Float through your portal into your heart. Your consciousness flows through your heart into your body. Take three deep, slow breaths. You are now fully back in your reality. Wiggle and stretch your body, then open your eyes.

Journal Work

Imagine for a moment that you have gone beyond human life and are now a single point of light having a conversation with another point of light. Discuss what you miss about having a human body on the physical plane. What do you think you would miss? Write and draw a list of all the things you enjoy about your physical body. Then, write or draw what you enjoy these things for.

Reflections and Actions

Whenever you walk through a doorway, imagine walking through the space between thoughts and be open to insights that will drop into your mind. They'll likely occur when you least expect them, such as during a shower, bath, driving, walking, or at the gym, as well as meditation or dreaming.

Are you ready for a change, like a new job, partner, lifestyle, or body? Or maybe you're waiting for resources to help you achieve your goals? We often say we want something different, but stepping away from our familiar routines can cause apprehension and lead to self-sabotage. Try something new that's just slightly outside your comfort zone. It doesn't have to be hard.

Here are some tips to help you try new experiences.

- Count your breaths and apply mindfulness techniques.
- Challenge your 'what if' thoughts. These take you into the future and create anxiety.
- Recall at least ten things you appreciate about yourself.
- Recall a few ways you become stronger after overcoming difficulties.
- Change your perspective.
- Make any task personally relevant — attach it to your higher values.

Research the phenomena called 'flow' or 'being in the flow state'. Mihaly Csikszentmihalyi, a Hungarian–American psychologist, was a co-founder of positive psychology and the first to identify and research flow. You may also enjoy the work of Steven Kotler, a flow researcher who has written many books. My favourite is *The Art of Impossible*.

40. MULTI-DIMENSIONAL

Simultaneous existence in numerous realms.

Each dimension lights up with its perspective of your desire, like an internal list of pros and cons that provides information to empower your decisions.

Message

Your awareness is stretching, and your vibrations are rising to include other dimensions. They will reveal multiple layers of fresh information on subjects and events in your life. Your curiosity, questions, and willingness to improve your life create this paradigm shift.

Each dimension resonates at unique frequencies, all coexisting within your space. Tuning in to these frequencies allows for varied perspectives and understandings of reality as you shift your vibration. You measure and translate your world from a three-dimensional view by representing time as past, present, and future, and space as height, depth, and width. However, you know things exist that you can't perceive. You access other dimensions when you sense a loved one around but they are not physically present. Doubt sets in if you turn to look or wonder if it was real. You are back in third-dimension perception, where these experiences aren't measurable.

The only way to go through other dimensions is through the heart. Direct your attention inward to your centre of unconditional love, knowingness, and bliss. Create a point of stillness by appreciating all this life has to offer. Your vibration will rise to take in the frequencies of other dimensions. The feelings of the heart intuitively translate the vibrations so the mind can process the information to understand it.

As you expand your awareness of reality, the feeling is so incredible and freeing that you may want others to experience this also. Everyone is at different levels of perception, which are perfect for them now. Your job is to feel, learn, and integrate all dimensional perspectives and truths while being grounded in your everyday life, enjoying the company of, and co-creation with, others. Allow your soul light to shine through you and inspire others to choose to see the world differently, if they so desire. Whatever they decide is up to them. You have the choice to love all through the many dimensions of perception.

Explore the exercises in the masterclass to embody the message and experience other dimensions.

Conscious Creator Masterclass: Experience Multiple Viewpoints

The previous masterclass explained the cyclical nature of creation, of letting go to create more. This masterclass introduces the concept of multidimensionality and brings more fulfilling information to create satisfying desires.

Visualisation

Find a comfortable place to sit or lie down. Place the *Multidimensional* card at your feet. In your mind, repeat your manifestation name or the word 'many' nine times. Gently close your eyes. Sense your body and concentrate on your breathing. Follow your breath inward. Hold for five seconds. Breathe out and release all tension. Relax and breathe naturally.

Imagine being pulled towards a beautiful, misty, coloured light with the qualities of harmony and security. The light enfolds you with a feeling of relaxation and peace. A shimmering cloak with the card's image printed on it gradually materialises out of the misty light. Take the cloak and wrap it around you.

The cloak vibrates with many dimensional frequencies. You are sensing all points of view at the same time, like multiple movies all screening simultaneously, but you are aware of them and know precisely what is happening in each one. It feels exciting and lovely. The vibrations become stronger and stronger and then suddenly stop. The inner movies continue playing way off in the distance, but you are still fully aware of each one. You look down at your hands and are surprised they are shimmering light. Surveying your body, you notice it, too, is glowing. You are experiencing your multidimensional self.

You notice a bright light on the earth and realise it is your physical self. As you observe your physical self, you are amazed at how you can sense all emotions, thoughts, and ideas flowing through your mind. Think of this unique perspective as a fact-finding expedition to help you understand what is going on in your mind. What viewpoints are you utilising in creating your life? Gently observe yourself, without judgement, for at least one minute as you allow this information to help you get better at creating your life.

When ready, remove the cloak and return it to the misty light. Feel yourself gently moving downwards into your body, bringing the information you have just gathered. Allow the light of harmony and security to stay with you for as long as you like. Take two deep breaths in and out. Wiggle your toes and fingers, stretch your body, and open your eyes.

Journal Work
After the visualisation, write or draw about the most prominent thing you perceived. Then write or illustrate how changing your perspective will help manifest your desires quickly.

Reflections and Actions
The shape of your consciousness will determine your perspective. For instance, an egg-shaped consciousness will allow an egg-shaped awareness of a movie you watch. When you expand your consciousness to the shape of a soccer ball, your comprehension will fit more understanding. As you develop your consciousness, you will experience other dimensional perceptions. It may seem trippy, but you are safe to explore all points of view.

Experience other dimensional perspectives with a crystal and flower
You will need a flower (or something from nature, such as a leaf) and a crystal for this exercise.

Pick up the crystal in your right hand. Thank it for being present and for the opportunity to learn something new about yourself through it. Imagine this crystal has a message for you and sense the subtle energies flowing from it. Allow wisdom and love to flow between you both for about a minute and take note of any messages that come to you.

Pick up the flower in your left hand. Thank it for being here and the opportunity to learn something new about yourself through its eyes. Imagine this flower has a message for you and sense the subtle energies flowing from it. Allow wisdom and love to flow between you both for about a minute and take note of any messages that arise.

Transfer the crystal to your left hand and the flower to your right. Sense the difference in energy between the crystal and the flower. Allow wisdom and love to flow for about a minute and take note of any messages you receive.

Gives thanks to the flower and the crystal for the multi-dimensional conversation.

Next time you are in nature, use this exercise with a tree, rock, or anything that catches your attention. There is wisdom all around you waiting to co-create and share.

41. NATURE WISDOM

Co-create with the natural world.

∞

Nature and plants hold wisdom to help you live authentically. Connecting with nature brings peace, balance, and inspiration, fostering your true self and supporting future generations through a shared lifeforce.

Message

Trees, nature, and plants want to connect with you—they have wisdom to share that can help you. The insights of the natural world have faded from the forefront of the collective mind, but they re-emerge when you seek a life filled with authentic experiences and manifestations. Nature holds no judgment, offering an environment where you can feel your true self.

Visit a forest, bush, or garden, or even place your hands around a potted plant. To connect deeply with the earth, lie down on the ground (sitting up connects you with your higher self). Thank the plants for the oxygen they provide and listen with an open mind as they thank you for the carbon dioxide you give them. The essence of this symbiotic relationship brings peace, balance, and remembrance. Allow this connection to fill you, then visualise it flowing from your feet—whether you are lying or sitting—into the earth. By intentionally grounding yourself, you create a solid foundation that empowers you to pursue your soul's desires. From this grounded perspective, plant your ideas and dreams into the earth to be realised through your physical senses.

The image on this card depicts Mount Shasta, a dormant volcano in California, USA. This and other magical natural places, connected by ley lines, make up the planet's electromagnetic field. Visiting these mystical locations heightens your awareness of love and wellbeing, triggering deeper insights into your soul's journey and collaborative connection with the earth. Remember, the same lifeforce that animates you flows through all of nature. As a custodian of your body and the body of nature, you are co-creating a new world for future generations.

Explore the exercises in the masterclass to embody the message and receive messages from the natural world.

Conscious Creator Masterclass: A Journey to Mount Shasta

The previous masterclass provided an experience of multi-dimensionality. This masterclass introduces the concept that we are nature.

This visualisation includes beings called 'merlins'. They are a group of beings that help humanity bypass stuck, conditioned patterns and unleash codes of inspired thinking and actions. This might seem like magic because you are unsure how to manifest beyond your emotions, choices, and conditioning. But soon, you will activate a level of information that will innovate new ways of manifestation. We can't change the future by blaming the past.

Visualisation

Find a comfortable place to sit or lie down. Place the *Nature Wisdom* card at your feet. In your mind, repeat your manifestation name or the word 'nature' nine times. Gently close your eyes. Sense your body and concentrate on your breathing. Follow your breath inward. Hold for five seconds. Breathe out and release all tension. Relax and breathe naturally.

In your mind's eye, take yourself to a beautiful natural place and find a spot to lie down. Take a deep breath in and feel the trees, plants, water, sky, and grass, and feel the breath of life flowing into you. As you exhale, feel the trees and plants inhale as they transform your carbon dioxide into oxygen for you to breathe in. Relax into this special co-creation that supports and nurtures you both.

Imagine you are sinking into the earth and travelling to a place that resonates with your heart and soul. Deep within your truth, your soul light travels on waves and frequencies emitted by ley lines and portals. Time and space melt away, and you arrive at a place in nature that feels like home. You are amazed to find yourself floating among beautiful, harmonic sound waves and other dimensional layers that project colours, sacred geometry, light beings, star beings, and flying machines.

A violet light descends from above, and many merlins appear. They float towards you, informing you telepathically that the

Merlin you know from myths is only one of many. The merlins and violet light surround you with a safe and peaceful feeling while transporting you to a colossal portal, whirling with light streams. They tell you this portal leads to interdimensional communities wanting to share information with you. It also connects with other portals that swirl within all other sacred places on Earth. Today is your introduction. When you are ready, they will be your guide.

The merlins and violet light surround and lift you upwards. Use your intention to gently travel back to your body on the waves and frequencies of ley lines and portals. You arrive at your physical body. As your light body floats above your physicality, tenderly observe the beauty of your body and send it loving gratitude for all it does for you. Breathe deeply and bring yourself back into your body. Your mind, body, soul, and spirit are now aligned, ready to create from a new level of consciousness. Take two deep breaths in and out. Wiggle your toes and fingers, stretch your body, open your eyes, and smile.

Journal Work

Write or draw any images, messages, colours, feelings, or impulses you experienced in the visualisation. Then, jot down or illustrate three things you are inspired to do in nature that feel fun.

Reflections and Actions

Try growing your own herbs, vegetables, and fruit, or create a community garden. Learning to grow food and sharing food with others are beautiful ways to honour our bodies and cultivate an abundance of nourishment.

Plant a tree so that humans and trees can co-create for future generations.

Research low-waste lifestyles. Incorporate as many ways as possible into your daily life.

Explore the ideas around regenerative, sustainable practices — a proactive approach with the goal of enhancing and revitalising the natural environment while helping reduce the negative impact on the environment. To find out more, you may like to research: regenerative agriculture, organic farming, and permaculture.

To explore a different approach to co-creating with the earth, I recommend reading Charles Eisenstein's *Climate: A New Story*.

42. INTERSPECIES COMMUNICATION

A unique, intuitive way to co-create.

Life is life. Everything flows from the same source, manifesting as distinct species with varying intentions for growth and experience. Being open to other points of view clarifies your desires. We are all one.

Message

You are ready to access dolphin wisdom about breath and sound. It is time to breathe new life into your dreams and desires. When you breathe out, push the air from the bottom of your lungs where fear becomes stuck. What sounds are your inner words carrying? Are they making way for, or hindering, the flow of your dreams? Improve your flow by introducing words representing your dreams to your internal dialogue and breathing out any obstacles.

Dolphins are beautiful creatures and mammals, just like you and me. It makes sense that we interpret their communications through the filter of human feelings and psychology. But this can lead to misunderstandings; dolphins aren't human. Open your heart and mind to a new, different way to communicate. Interspecies communication applies the idea that all life—including fauna, flora, minerals, elements, planets, stars, moons, galaxies, humans, and extraterrestrial beings—flows from the same source. The energy that flows through you also flows through all other life forms. We are all streams of consciousness with differing intentions for growth and experience.

Explore the exercises in the masterclass to embody the message and connect with another species.

Conscious Creator Masterclass: Intuitively Connecting with an Animal Friend

The previous masterclass unveiled the mystical wisdom of nature, emphasising the importance of listening and engaging with it. This masterclass introduces a way to communicate with animals and other species in a generous and courteous space, fostering more extraordinary co-creations.

Choose an animal that you would like to connect and communicate with. Your animal friend doesn't have to be in the same room as you; they are natural meditators and will easily connect with you wherever they are.

Visualisation

Place the *Interspecies Communication* card at your feet. Gently close your eyes. In your mind, repeat your manifestation name or the word 'connect' nine times. Sense your body and concentrate on your breathing. Follow your breath inward. Hold for five seconds. Breathe out and release all tension. Relax. Open your heart and mind to the following words:

> *We are all one. Life is life. Everything flows from the same source, manifesting as different species. Allow your mind to let go and be at peace with yourself and all living things.*

In your mind's eye, take yourself to a beautiful natural place and find a spot to sit. Relax and align with your balanced centre to reveal your unique energy, which converts into a golden, loving light. Animals predominantly sense you through the energy you emit.

Your animal friend is here. Invite them to sit or lie with you. Feel them settle and relax. Feel their unique, golden, loving light. Sense the words "this feels good" inside you. It feels like a natural conversation with yourself, but you know you didn't say the words. This was your animal friend talking to you. You have tuned into their frequency and can now receive and intercept their energetic impulses.

Feel the energetic connection between the two of you. Allow your animal friend to share intuitive wisdom. Let them remind you that all living creatures are much more than you think they are, including you. Stay in communication with your animal friend for at least one minute. Enjoy.

When you are ready to leave, say goodbye to your animal friend and watch as they disappear into the distance. A golden, misty light springs up and encircles you; it is the new relationship that the two of you created. Take this back into your world as you breathe golden, misty light into your body. Be fully present in your body by breathing deeply. Wiggle your toes and fingers. Then stretch your body and open your eyes.

Journal Work

When you have finished the visualisation, write or draw any messages, colours, feelings, or impulses you received to ground and refine the communication. Then, write or draw about where in your body you felt any messages, colours, feelings, or impulses you received. It might be your heart, stomach, throat, or somewhere else. Your body is unlocking new ways to communicate for the fun of it.

Reflections and Actions

Because an animal doesn't speak your language, we must learn to communicate differently. For instance, how would you ask where a toilet is if you were in a foreign country and didn't speak the language? The next time you are around an animal, visualise introducing yourself with kindness and curiosity. Send it to the animal's heart for about 30 seconds and see what happens.

When animals shake, they release overwhelming or traumatic events to return to a balanced way of being. If they ran around in a fearful state, they would be skittish and easy pickings for predators. The next time you feel overwhelmed or have an excess of negative energy, do what an animal does — shake it off. Try swinging your arms around, wiggle your hips vigorously, then flick your arms. Imagine you see any excess negative energy flying from your fingertips. Keep going for about 30 seconds. Then, write or draw in your journal how you felt and feel now.

43. ALTERNATE LIFETIMES

Clarify desires with wisdom from your soul experiences.

This beautiful life is one of many experiences your soul will have as it journeys through the universe, gaining clarity about your desires. Experiences reveal and integrate your dreams so they don't remain unrealised fantasies.

MESSAGE

You are receiving glimpses of other lives to help you make the most of this life. Whatever you need to know to help you heal or embrace and discover more of your authentic self will come to you through dreams, meditations, déjà vu, or sparks of interest in a historical period. Your present life is important and precious and you are learning how to get better at your life. This is one of many lives that make up your soul.

Your mind accesses an increased bandwidth of frequencies and information as your awareness expands. Your mind can now receive and translate this information. The akashic records serve as a universal network intertwining all dimensions and life experiences. They offer insights into past, present, and future possibilities for understanding one's soul journey. Sensing alternate realities can bring ideas and experiences for healing and understanding to your mind. In the beginning, you will likely experience these emotionally, which is the easiest way to convey large amounts of information.

To distinguish between your various lifetimes, imagine your soul is a hard drive. When you let go of a physical life, it is archived as a file on your soul's hard drive. Anyone who knew you in that life or a past life will recognise you because the file holds the qualities and flavour of you in that life. But that isn't all you are — you are so much more. Everything behind you is history, and everything in front of you is a mystery. You are here, now, on the crest of a soul-light wave, riding it for the sheer joy of it. All that has ever been rides the wave of expansion with you.

Explore the exercises in the masterclass to embody the message and experience other existences you have experienced.

Conscious Creator Masterclass: Experience Another Life

The previous masterclass provided a way to communicate with animals and other species in a generous and courteous space, fostering more extraordinary co-creations. This masterclass introduces the viewpoints of different incarnations to assist you in creating an authentic life.

Visualisation

Find a comfortable place to sit, place the *Alternate Lives* card at your feet and rest your hands on your lap. In your mind, repeat your manifestation name or the word 'being' nine times. Close your eyes. Focus on the middle of your chest and imagine you are walking on a magical path leading to your mind's inner landscape. Concentrate all your attention inward. Relax and breathe.

Imagine a door in your mind. It is a magical door that will lead you to an alternate life that you have lived. Push the door open and step through into a remembrance of a life lived. It feels safe. You are here to observe and collate information that will help you find solutions and inspiration in your present life. Take deep breaths. Allow some time to reorient yourself to your surroundings.

Walk through this life and explore wherever you feel drawn to. If you feel emotional at any point, take a breath and ask what it wants to share, then take another breath and go back to exploring and observing. Stay in this life story for at least five minutes.

When you feel ready, thank this life for the experience and for sharing its memories. Walk back through the magical door of time that brought you here. Return to the present by counting down from five to one. On reaching one, you are back in your life right now. Wiggle your toes and fingers. Take a deep breath, fully stretch your body, and open your eyes. Welcome back to your magnificent life.

Journal Work

After the visualisation, write or draw the answers to these questions. As well as expanding your consciousness and opening your mind to different planes of existence, this journal writing will help you fine-tune the desires you want to experience in life.

- What did the landscape look like? Were you in nature, or a city or town?
- Were you wearing shoes? If so, what type?
- What were you wearing?
- Was your body masculine or feminine? Were you human?
- How did you feel? Were you happy, sad, strong, or weak?
- Were there others around you, and did you recognise anyone from your present life?
- Who were your friends or family? Did you feel any emotions connected to them?
- Where did you live? What did it look like? Did you live with anyone?
- How did you feel about your home and those around you?
- Did you see what you did for a job or what you did each day? How did you feel about your daily routine? Was it fulfilling?
- Was there a significant event? If so, how did you feel about it?
- Where did the story of this life end?

Reflections and Actions

Receive any information gently by allowing it to join your mind and expand your consciousness slowly. If it doesn't make sense, let it be a part of your mind reference, as if you were buying a book you are yet to read. More information may come to you through a meditation, dream, overheard conversation, movie, song, download, channelling, or through a therapist.

Read books or watch movies that explore different or alternate timelines and time travel. Some good examples of TV and movies are:

- *Outlander*, the TV series and books
- *12 Monkeys*, the movie and TV series
- The *Back to the Future* trilogy (1980s)
- *Sliding Doors* (1998)
- *Yesterday* (2019)

Open your imagination to the experiences of alternate lives by going into nature and imagining what it would be like to be a bird, a leaf, a tree, an insect, a raindrop, the wind, the sun, or the soil. This is a form of shapeshifting. It is an insightful practice that lifts your mind beyond the physical, into your sensing reality. The same lifeforce energy that flows through you, flows through all sentient beings and life. When you align with your energy, you have access to energy everywhere. From this loving space, you can become one with anything you focus on.

44. ETERNITY

An unfurling space.

Your soul doesn't exist in you; it is you, eternal. You will always recognise yourself, even when you release your body. Now that you know you can't die, you can live, and create, this beautiful, precious life to its fullest.

Message

A new sense of freedom is resetting your nervous system, and soon you will have greater trust in your ability to direct your choices. Inspire yourself to venture into new experiences without needing to know the outcome. The unknown scares us because we believe that we won't recognise ourselves if we change. But you will always be you.

Your soul is eternal — it doesn't die. You will let go of this body one day. You will always recognise yourself. This message is to help you live your life to the fullest. The playing field of life is unlimited and loving. There is so much space to create infinite manifestations.

When your soul asked to be more, you incarnated into this form to explore physical life. You are the inner observer who experiences the world through your mind and body as it alters and grows. Even though your thoughts, feelings, and intelligence will change, your soul is eternal. It is a pure, loving feeling in your heart that you can come home to whenever you want, a place to balance and reset your frequency to your authentic self.

Explore the exercises in the masterclass to embody the message and experience a feeling of infinite eternity.

Conscious Creator Masterclass: Discover Your Eternal Nature

The previous masterclass explained the concept of your many incarnations and their viewpoints to help you create authentic desires for this life. This masterclass introduces the eternal nature of your soul and the universe, and how to surrender your mind to your heart.

Visualisation

Find a comfortable place to sit, place the *Eternity* card at your feet and rest your hands on your lap. In your mind, repeat your manifestation name or the word 'continue' nine times. Gently close your eyes and imagine you are sitting on soft, green grass, with your back leaning against a tree trunk. Breathe deeply and slowly.

Gradually allow yourself to merge with the energy of the tree, your breath matching its breathing. Experience the tree letting go to become more. Observe the leaves turning yellow, orange, and red. Watch as they begin to fall from the tree on a gentle autumn breeze.

Watch one leaf release itself from the tree. It has been nurtured over the past season and is now ready to transform. It releases from the tree and drifts like a feather to the waiting arms of Mother Earth. She embraces the brave leaf, welcoming it into the eternal, loving embrace of all. Here, the leaf connects to all things and becomes part of the rich soil where new seeds are planted and grow.

Imagine you are the next leaf to release itself. Feel yourself float on the gentle breeze, knowing this is the next chapter of your life. You are greeted with a loving hug from Mother Earth, who draws you into her inner world. Feel a transformation occurring. You have become part of the nourishing soil, awaiting a seed you can nourish. You are still you, just with a beautiful new task. Float here for at least two minutes.

When you are ready, breathe deeply and return to your body. Honour all you have achieved as you feel yourself flowing into your physical form. You no longer cling to whatever you have previously created and accomplished — let it all go. Move on and create more. Thank the leaf and tree for your experience. Be here now in the unfolding journey into the infinite wonderment of you. Focus on your breath. Wiggle your toes and fingers. Then stretch your body and open your eyes to eternity.

Journal Work

After the visualisation, take yourself back to the leaf you became. As the leaf, write or draw what you saw, felt, heard, and smelt. You are activating your ability to empathise without judging. This is a form of shapeshifting.

Reflections and Actions

Eternity is a difficult concept for our minds to grasp, as our brains are used to thinking in terms of linear time — past, present, and future. We can mistake the term 'eternity' to mean a very long time. However, it is outside of time, which seems incomprehensible.

To Create a Sense of Eternity

Draw an eternity symbol over your chest eight times as you breathe deeply. Place both hands on your chest, close your eyes, and keep drawing it in your mind for another eight times. Then focus on the point in the middle of the symbol. Stay here for at least two minutes. Open your eyes when you are ready. You have calibrated your frequency to your soul, and your soul is eternal.

Mind-Expanding Exercises

Visit the Garden of Cosmic Speculation in Holywood, Scotland. It is a 30-acre garden inspired by the principles of modern physics.

Check out the work of artist M.C. Escher (1898–1972). He was a Dutch graphic artist known for his iconic optical illusions.

Explore the Möbius strip, a unique surface created by twisting a long, narrow strip of material 180 degrees and connecting its ends, resulting in a one-sided, continuous surface. Below are instructions on how to make and play with one. You will need a piece of paper and a small piece of adhesive tape.

1. Cut a thin strip of paper about 2.5cm or 1 inch wide and any length.
2. Gently twist one of the ends 180 degrees, or one half-twist.
3. Bring the ends together and fasten them with the tape, creating a ring with a half-twist inside.
4. Then, take a finger and run it over the sides of the strip. Keep going, and don't take your finger off. You'll eventually move all the way around both sides, back to where you began.

45. PASSION CREATOR

Crafting a new world from your highest potential.

When you are open to the possibility that all is possible and then surrender what you perceive as reality into the limitless imagination of your soul, you become a passionate creator with absolute certainty that anything is possible.

Message

Your passion creator is awakening, and soon you will encounter inspired ideas in your nightdreams, daydreams, or meditations. Evolved pathways and kind experiences for you and everyone else will reveal themselves to you. You are a part of the new world. Gratitude and compassion for humanity, animals, nature, or the earth are the keys to unlocking a flow of creative inspiration that ripples outward to inspire others to awaken their heartfulness.

You have lowered the shield around your heart, and feelings are rushing in. You may have forgotten how intense sensations and feelings unbalance your nervous system. But keep letting the feeling in. They will transmute into loving wonderment and inspired action when they reach intensity. In the past, you may have mistaken this intensity as sadness, any feeling of the unknown for fear, and any sense of peace for boredom. But now you can use these feelings as a gateway to your magical inner world and direct access to your passion creator.

You are the custodian of your body, mind, and soul. By valuing yourself, you inspire others to embrace their authentic selves. Instead of worrying about the future, focus on how you'll navigate it. If you aim to accumulate experiences, the point of this is not to become a better critic—often mistaken for wisdom—but to cultivate love and receive it in return.

Explore the exercises in the masterclass to embody the message and awaken your passion creator.

Conscious Creator Masterclass: Limitless Creating

The previous masterclass introduced the idea of the eternal nature of your soul, the universe, and the infinite space for your creations. This masterclass introduces your passion creator as the driver of your soul's eternal desires.

Visualisation
Find a comfortable place to sit down. Place the *Passion Creator* card at your feet and rest your hands on your lap. In your mind, repeat your manifestation name or the word 'invent' nine times. Gently close your eyes. Sense your body and concentrate on your breathing. Take your focus to the middle of your chest and sense a

peaceful, calm pulse deep within your heart. Your heart grows and expands until it surrounds you in profound love and boundless visions. You begin to radiate your soul light.

Floating into the cosmos deep within your heart, you become the energy that creates stars. Your being drifts within beautiful, colourful clouds of hydrogen and stardust. You are a part of the creative heart of the universe, ready to become more. The idea that you are prepared causes a vibrational shift that charges your particles of desire. You begin to fluctuate, and your form is moving towards destiny.

Deep within colourful clouds, the dance of stars commences. Your charged particles spiral towards and away from each other, coming together and moving apart until you find your complementary partner. You unite in an explosion of love and light to become one, then fall in on each other to birth a point of light.

Within this light, a message flows into your consciousness:

There is a version of this world you dream about, where you stand on the brink of greatness. Your life has brought you to this moment. Oversee your destiny and build your own life. Your heart is the inspiration and key to true desires. Your mind organises the desires into 'wouldn't it be lovely' scenarios. The desire expands, and your body vibrates with emotion. Your felt sense becomes a wave of vibrations, entirely existing in the non-physical realm. Momentum is building. Components needed to manifest your desire are magnetically and magically drawn towards it.

You feel your desire as if it is here with you now. Integrate the knowing. It becomes fully formed in your whole being, as if you have already experienced it. Ready yourself to receive your desire and its many variations by smiling.

Enjoy your life on the way to all you desire. Be curious, question your motivations, self-inquire, and heal. Discover your joy and share it with others. Seek to love and understand all that we judge, especially ourselves, compassionately. We are all brothers and sisters, walking each other home.

Float here for at least two minutes as the message merges with you.

When you feel ready, focus on your breath. Each breath draws your heart closer to your physical body. Move into matter and slide gently into your physicalness. This experience establishes deep within the idea that all your dreams already exist. Everything you have ever desired is already in existence, waiting for you to become an energetic match to draw it into your reality. How amazing and empowering is that to know? That you create your reality.

Focus on your breath. Wiggle your toes and fingers. Then, stretch your body and open your eyes to a new Earth.

Journal Work

Having a big vision forms the blueprint, and writing it down becomes the scaffold, which you will fill in with inspired actions. After the visualisation, write or draw what you want to create in your life. Then, write or draw what you would like to create to make life better for you and others.

Reflections and Actions

Each breath, each day, is an opportunity to tune in to our passion and create more of it. Imagine your key is your manifestation name. Inhale deeply and say your manifestation name. Feel your heart unlocking as you exhale. Your passions emerge like ribbons of coloured light to inspire curiosity and compassion. Take three deep breaths and then record your thoughts and feelings in your journal.

Act on or think about something you are passionate about, whether it is cooking, gardening, playing, reading, or something else. You know you are passionate about it when you feel present. Time seems to disappear, you smile inside, and you may feel a slight pleasant tingling, tension, or urgency. That is your passion creator celebrating.

Allow all experiences to come to you for the wonderment of more creation. Push nothing away or pull anything towards you. Simply *be*, and you will know what to do. Whatever experience you are having at this moment is the most helpful for the evolution of your consciousness.

Magic and miracles exist. They are just elements science can't explain yet. When you anticipate miracles, more magic will flow into your vibrational experience. You are making the unknown known and creating a better world.

ABOUT THE AUTHOR

DENISE JARVIE is not just a soul coach and mentor, she's a guide to reconnecting with your true essence and unlocking the boundless potential within. With her warm demeanour and infectious sense of humour, she creates a nurturing environment where any topic can be explored with ease.

Born on November 11 near the mystical Stonehenge in the UK, Denise's journey led her to Melbourne, Australia, at a young age. Now residing in Sydney with her quirky Tonkinese cat, she embodies the vibrant energy of both hemispheres.

Having faced her own battles with anxiety and depression, Denise's personal transformation ignited a passion for understanding the human psyche. Over the past 25 years, she has delved into meditation, metaphysics, psychology, and healing, emerging as a beacon of wisdom and insight.

Denise's bestselling creations, including *The Secret Language of Light*, *The Secret Language of Darkness* and *The Tarot of Light*, reflect her profound understanding of spiritual principles and holistic healing. Her work encompasses a diverse range of titles, from meditations to oracles, all aimed at empowering individuals to embrace their authenticity and live their most fulfilling lives.

Beyond her literary achievements, Denise is a devoted cook, gardener, and fitness enthusiast. Whether she's crafting transformative content, coaching clients, or tending to her garden, she radiates an infectious zest for life.

Discover Denise's visionary work and embark on your own journey of self-discovery at www.denisejarvie.com

ABOUT THE ARTIST

Artistic talent combined with life-long exploration of consciousness and devotion to self-realisation has given DANIEL B. HOLEMAN an ability to depict uplifting and profound sacred imagery. His inspirational paintings often have a strong impact on people.

Daniel feels it is not so much the beauty but the place it stirs within which people respond to. He invites the viewer to dive into a deeper dimension of consciousness while viewing his paintings, allowing the high-frequency imagery to activate their higher frequencies within. The imagery activates forgotten awareness of a felt sense of HOME—a warm, familiar and heartfelt state of mind—and his videos are a deeply moving experience to behold.

Daniel's primary role in life is that of a messenger and guide for all (who are ready) to realise our Unity. He offers insight, clarity and counsel on living in this world with that awareness. And the art that comes through him is the creative expression of that role. He is a wayshower, helping others realise and live their unique higher purpose — their fullest potential, based on a foundation of Unity Consciousness and the Clarity of Being who we are designed to be and the role we are here to fill in life.

He is an Ambassador for the Gene Keys and Golden Path transformation tools and offers introduction and guidance. Website: www.AwakenVisions.com

ALSO AVAILABLE FROM BLUE ANGEL PUBLISHING®

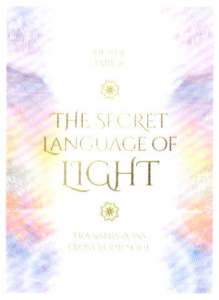

THE SECRET LANGUAGE OF LIGHT

Transmissions from your Soul

Denise Jarvie
Artwork by Daniel B. Holeman

The impulse to create and energise peace, love and fulfilment is alive within you. This glorious oracle works with the mysteries and secrets of the light to illuminate the rich possibility and potential inside you. The light is a constant guide and support, and its language inspires, empowers and activates your soul spark.

Step into the wonder of the light through the inspired insight of Denise Jarvie and the radiant artwork of Daniel B. Holeman to enliven the love, vision and strength of your heart. Access the wisdom of these stunning cards through the specifically designed meditations, reflections, and exercises for divination, contemplation, or revelation. You can also work through the 45 cards and detailed 164-page guidebook for a complete soul mastery class. The language of light speaks to eternity, to life, and to you. Tune into its secrets and shine!

ISBN: 978-1-925538-47-2
45 cards and 164-page guidebook.

ALSO AVAILABLE FROM BLUE ANGEL PUBLISHING®

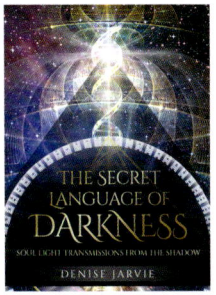

THE SECRET LANGUAGE OF DARKNESS

Soul Light Transmissions from the Shadow

Denise Jarvie
Artwork by Daniel B. Holeman

Unlock the secrets of your inner world with *The Secret Language of Darkness*. An inner repository of all the sensations and experiences you've disowned, your shadow is part of you, and it longs to be embraced and belong. These cards shine a light on your deepest shadows, guiding you towards wholeness and healing.

Discover the hidden messages and beliefs that hold you back from your best life. Through shadow mastery classes and insightful card messages, you'll gain the skills to face and integrate repressed aspects of your personality.

Each card holds a sacred message and an opportunity for self-discovery, leading you on a journey of liberation and self-awareness. Step into the realm of shadow work and unleash the power of your authentic self.

ISBN: 978-1-922574-16-9
45 cards and 216-page guidebook.

ALSO AVAILABLE FROM BLUE ANGEL PUBLISHING®

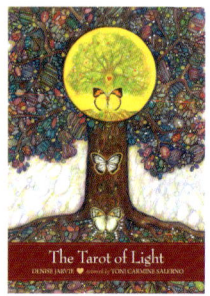

THE TAROT OF LIGHT

Denise Jarvie
Artwork by Toni Carmine Salerno

Tarot is a path of self-knowing that unveils the mysteries that lie before and within us. The divine and loving messages within *The Tarot of Light* offer a balanced view of past, present and future, so your readings bring illumination, learning, insight and direction for a brighter, lighter tomorrow.

Denise Jarvie brings a contemporary approach to traditional tarot that features seventy-eight of Toni Carmine Salerno's most enchanting artworks. The suits of the minor arcana have become Angels (Swords), Hearts (Cups), Stars (Wands), and Trees (Pentacles) to align with the themes that run through Toni's work. Denise also revisits the 22 cards of the major arcana, so they reflect modern-day archetypes. These cards hold divine and loving energy to encourage harmonious perceptions and help you manifest your hopes, dreams and desires. Don't just see the future, co-create it!

ISBN: 978-0-6487467-2-0
78 cards and 120-page guidebook.

ALSO AVAILABLE FROM BLUE ANGEL PUBLISHING®

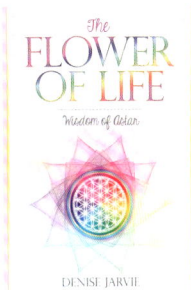

THE FLOWER OF LIFE

Wisdom of Astar

Denise Jarvie

The Flower of Life contains the seed of all possibilities, the essence of all desire. This powerful creative symbol which lends its name to this deck and graces the back of each card within it holds infinite divine potential. These cards are a portal to connect you with that very potential locked deep within you. Take a journey with Astar, a wise, loving energetic consciousness whose energy permeates this deck with incredible wisdom and insights to share to help you remember your true beauty and worth. Here is a star map of your potential. Astar holds the faith of your love and truth even when you have forgotten and constantly streams it to you through the light of our day star – the Sun and the sparkling stars at night.

ISBN: 978-1-922161-26-0
52 guidance cards and booklet.

Notes

Notes

For more information on this
or any Blue Angel Publishing release,
please visit our website at:

www.BlueAngelOnline.com